ASIAN VEGAN COOKING

*A
High-Energy
Approach to
Healthy Living*

KIM LE, Ph.D.

Sterling Publishing Co., Inc.
New York

Library of Congress Cataloging-in-Publication Data
Available upon Request.

2 4 6 8 10 9 7 5 3

Published 2003 by Sterling Publishing Co., Inc.
387 Park Avenue South, New York, NY 10016
Originally published by Rudra Press under the title *High Energy
Living: Vegetarian Cooking for Health* © 1997 by Kim Le
Distributed in Canada by Sterling Publishing
℅ Canadian Manda Group, One Atlantic Avenue, Suite 105
Toronto, Ontario, Canada M6K 3E7
Distributed in Great Britain by Chrysalis Books
64 Brewery Road, London N7 9NT, England
Distributed in Australia by Capricorn Link (Australia) Pty. Ltd.
P.O. Box 704, Windsor, NSW 2756, Australia

Sterling ISBN-1-4027-0627-8

Contents

RECIPES FOR
HIGH-ENERGY LIVING

*This book is dedicated to
all those seeking a healthier life
and a more compassionate path.*

Preface

I grew up in Vietnam during a time of severe depression in that country. My health was always very fragile, due in part to being a premature baby. My grandmother, who was my closest friend, encouraged me to practice vegetarianism as part of a healthful and compassionate way of living and eating.

At any early age, I resisted eating meat; the thought, sight, or smell was disagreeable to me. However, due to my poor constitution, many health practitioners advised me to consume meat in order to sustain my strength. This recommendation seemed logical at the time, and to please my parents I gave in and consumed meat and fish. During those youthful years I struggled with my diet, going back and forth with myself about my health and my beliefs.

As time went on, my war-torn country and my own poor health motivated me to become a healer. As I observed my patients and pursued extensive research about the nutritional aspects of vegetarianism, I once again became determined to abstain from animal foods. Since eliminating animal products from my diet many years ago, the fragile health condition stemming from my childhood has disappeared. My energy has become more stable, my mind more clear, and my dreams more vivid.

We humans are small universes within a larger universe. Life involves constant exchange between these universes. As we reside in the larger universe so it also resides in us. With such an understanding, we appreciate the fact that within us, we possess the natures of all beings. The old adage goes "We are what we eat." In this light, in addition to being part of a healthy lifestyle, vegetarianism can also be seen as a life of compassion in action.

Acknowledgments

Sincere thanks go to numerous good spiritual friends without whom this book would not have reach completion. Heading the list are my parents who brought me into this life; it is due to their suffering and hardship that I have chosen a life of service to others.

Thanks go to Christine Hoffman (Tara) and Lai Chee for their encouragement and work on the manuscript as well as their contributions of cooking knowledge and recipes. Their sincerity and devotion are reflected throughout the book.

Thank you to John Gorman (Norbu) for his great data-processing knowledge and untiring assistance in bringing this book to fruition.

And finally, thanks to the editorial and production staffs at Rudra Press for all their fine work.

May all who encounter this book experience inner peace and clarity of mind as they follow the path of healthy and compassionate eating.

Introduction

During twenty years of work in the healing professions, I have carefully observed my patients' patterns of physical, emotional, and mental imbalance. From my research and experience, it is apparent that patients' symptoms are linked to the foods they consume and the lifestyles they follow. I have concluded that we create illness, illness doesn't create us. To treat disease is to treat what is dead—to heal ourselves is to treat what is alive.

When we are sick, we seek one form of treatment after another in an attempt to cure our symptoms. As we search to understand our illnesses, we read and study more and more about disease and further burden our minds. Eventually we might deteriorate and die with feelings of confusion, desperation, and hopelessness. Medical tests, procedures, and analytical thinking will not provide ultimate healing. Only when we stop blaming external conditions and instead turn inward to look deeply within ourselves do we realize that disease doesn't just manifest from thin air or from anything outside ourselves.

When we understand this, we can begin to change our diet, our way of thinking and behaving, and even our motivation for living. Without such inner effort, we continue to suffer physically and emotionally while exhausting our energy and finances on symptomatic cures. However, illness can be transformed by developing a new attitude and living a simpler life. In fact, changing our lifestyle can miraculously alter the course of even a serious illness like cancer.

Western culture has been slow to teach the concepts and benefits of preventive medicine and self-healing. Most Western treatments are tailored to the analysis of symptoms relating to a specific organ or area of the body rather than to a holistic approach. If a treatment does not consider the whole interplay of body, mind, and emotions, then even if symptoms are cured, sickness will lie dormant only to manifest another time and perhaps in a different part of the body.

Our bodies are magnificent, though unreliable, machines. They can break down at any time and certainly have no permanence. Undeniably, as we grow older, our bodies will decline in one way or another until we die. The same is true of the mind; for most of us the mind is not reliable or steady. It can be a slave to damaging habits, often dwelling in memories of the past or desires for the future. The mind is easily swayed by emotional currents and can be both deceived and deceptive.

By eating properly and disciplining our minds, we can live the healthiest and fullest life possible in body, mind, emotions, and spirit. In this way, we benefit ourselves and everyone we have contact with.

Eating right is more easily said than done. All of us have attempted to change our diet at some time and probably found it to be quite difficult. But over the long term, unless you embrace and adhere to a wholesome, nutritious diet, you will eventually suffer the consequences of depleted energy and poor health. You can undertake the rewarding effort of understanding nutrition and eating well or you can pay doctors and hospitals to try and alleviate your symptoms and cure your illnesses. The choice is yours.

A nutritious diet is vital to any process of healing. It requires minimal expense compared to many treatment methods. If we wait until a serious or terminal illness becomes apparent, we may be faced with huge medical bills, great disappointment, and irreversible pain. It might not be possible to change everything at once, but if we begin now and use each meal as a step on the ladder to optimum health, then we have successfully started on a healing path.

This book contains vital messages for healthy living through simple diet and cooking. It is written from years of accumulated knowledge as a health practitioner as well as from personal experience in the choices I have made for daily living. The material included enables us to expand our potential to heal ourselves through good nutrition and preparation of simple, tasty vegetarian dishes.

THE FUNDAMENTALS OF HIGH-ENERGY LIVING

Expanding Our
View of Health

According to ancient Oriental teachings and traditional Chinese medicine, the human body is a microcosm in the larger macrocosm of the universe. The universe contains sky and earth and the human body contains the two basic constituents of qi (chi) and blood. Nature is governed by five primordial forces that progress through five phases: Wood, Fire, Earth, Metal, and Water. Similarly, the human body is organized by five functional systems, the organ networks: liver, heart, spleen, lung, and kidney.

Our flesh, bones, hair, nails, tissues, and ligaments belong to the earth. Blood, urine, mucus, phlegm, tears, and sweat belong to the water element. The warmth of our body belongs to the fire element. Our breath and the flexibility behind each movement, from blinking our eyes to bending our joints, belong to the wind. The proper functioning of these networks is based on the harmonious flow between qi and blood.

According to this conception, health is determined by the quality and quantity of qi and blood along with the harmonious interaction of the five organ networks. Illness is the disturbance of the five organ networks and the disharmony between qi and blood. A human being is also much more than organs, blood, and qi; thought patterns and emotions inextricably link us with our physical environments and our spirit. Illness can result from disturbances in these links.

Qi is a difficult term to grasp—even Chinese medical practitioners have a hard time truly understanding it. Nothing can exist without qi. To begin to understand, we need to become totally aware of our own life and the life of everything around us. Qi is the dynamic quality responsible for all activity and life—it is life force. It initiates all pulsation and movement. Cognition, feeling, waking, sleeping, walking, digesting are all manifested by qi. Without qi, we cannot consume, transform, store, or transmit anything.

While qi is immaterial, blood is material. Blood expresses the quality and quantity of qi. Blood gives solidity to the shape that qi creates. Blood encompasses all structural and connective tissue in the body. Through qi, blood creates and maintains survival on the coarse level of existence.

Blood's nature is passive, inert, thick, and easily becomes stagnant. Qi is active, warm, and keeps the blood moving. Qi and blood work interdependently. Qi by itself has no material expression and no source for renewal. On the other hand, blood without qi is stagnant and dead. Blood goes wherever qi goes. It is said that blood is the mother of qi. Blood is also considered to be the material basis of the mind. If blood is stagnant, the mind becomes dull and confused.

Externally, the movements of the universe such as weather, natural catastrophes, war, and peace are bound by Heaven and Earth. Internally, the human organism is controlled by the intermingling of psyche and soma known as Shen and Essence. Shen is the eternal and is related to the immaterial expression of the individual; Essence deals with the body's material source. Essence is what we inherit from our past deeds, from our father and mother's genetic material, and from the environment in which we grow up.

Essence is what we are endowed with at birth. It is the basis of our growth, development, and reproduction. Essence imparts continuity of life through the reproductive and genetic material. Health or sickness is determined by Essence, which continuously changes based on the way we live and eat. Stress, over-exhaustion, excessive sexual activities, poor nutrition, and lack of exercise are detrimental to the quality of Essence.

Shen is the expression of life. It reflects the totality of an individual. It encompasses both the tangible and intangible realms of personal experience. When the mind is in harmony with the body, then the Shen of the individual radiates through spirit. In a subtle way, Shen is responsible for the integration among body, mind, and emotions.

In Chinese medicine, illness manifests from a disharmony of Shen, Essence, qi, or blood. Any problem needs to be approached holistically. The story below helps summarize how important it is to apply the concept of holistic healing in regard to all aspects of living and healing.

Ten years ago, when I was practicing Chinese medicine in Florida, there was a local writer who wished to do an article about me and my practice. He was in his mid-seventies but seemed vigorous and happy.

After interviewing me, he revealed that he had heard a lot of good things about my healing methods and he wanted to try them for himself. His complaint was pain and numbness in his right leg. I gave him a complete diagnosis, an explanation of his condition, and my recommendation for treatment. He understood and agreed to let me treat him.

A week later he returned for his second treatment. When I entered the treatment room, he said to me, "Doctor, last week when I was here I only wanted you to treat my right leg, but you inserted needles in both legs. Not only that, you spoke to me about my diet and my emotions. Just so you know, there is nothing wrong with my food intake and the pain in my leg has nothing to do with my feelings and emotions. Can you just take care of my leg problem and forget about the other issues?" I answered him, "Sure, I will treat only your leg if you can just leave your feelings and emotions home." I watched the light dawn as he sat back in his chair and said softly, "Oh, I see, you mean everything is connected."

In my practice, I find over and over that we are disconnected from the total integration of our bodies, minds, and emotions. We lose track of the fact that all of these things are impermanent and that they are best used to cultivate our spiritual development and to be of service to humankind. In this light, properly nourishing our bodies and disciplining our minds extends beyond our own health into service to our families, friends, communities, and the world at large.

The Benefits of
Being Vegetarian

Our stressful society and our busy lifestyles provide us very little time for reflection and deep contemplation. From infancy to adulthood we tend to follow along established patterns of living and thinking. Only when crisis strikes us or our loved ones do we begin to ask why.

Although we experience some level of suffering in our own lives, it's rare that we truly comprehend the suffering of others. When I came to America, I was shocked at the loving care people showered on their pets while they had total disregard for animals they consumed in the form of meat!

At my first welcome dinner with my American host, Kathy, I was bewildered as I witnessed a confusing scene. She was lovingly stroking her pet cat with her left hand while simultaneously using her right hand to put pieces of juicy pork chop in her mouth. I could not believe that she didn't recognize the similarity between the pet on her lap and the meat on her plate. After savoring her meal she looked up and found that I was staring at her.

Kathy asked why I wasn't eating. I tried to convey to her that I did not eat meat and hoped that would not cause conflict in our relationship. We began to talk about my experiences growing up in Vietnam, my culture, and so on. I could tell Kathy was concerned for my lack of understanding Western culture and habits. Of course, my broken English was no help in expressing my feelings and beliefs. At the time I felt very frustrated but we managed to get along well.

A year later, I received a phone call from Kathy informing me that she was diagnosed with terminal cancer and was given three months to live. At a time of desperation and hopelessness she asked if I could perform a miracle. With some reluctance I told her that a miracle was, in fact, within her reach only if she was willing to change. She concluded our conversation by saying, "I'll do anything if I can live."

Subsequently, she came to me to receive treatments and nutritional and lifestyle consultation. She was determined to get well, but I knew then that no matter how desperate a person might be, there is always a certain limit to what one can do. My goal was to help her, not to challenge her faith. Therefore, instead of asking her to become a vegetarian, I advised her to eat brown rice and roasted sesame seeds for six months.

She agreed to the schedule and stuck with the diet regime. As time went on, I carefully outlined what she could add to her diet and helped her with some recipes. Six months passed and Kathy was still alive. Not only was she cancer-free but she had more energy and was more mentally alert. However, she still didn't call herself a vegetarian.

One evening I was invited to her birthday party to celebrate her "extension of life." On the table was a birthday cake that was baked with natural ingredients by her friends as well as another plate that was carefully decorated but covered. I kept wondering what was inside.

After singing birthday wishes to her and cutting the cake, she picked up that big plate and walked over to me. I was full of anticipation as she handed the plate to me and said, "Thank you for saving my life. This present is specially made for you."

I was very touched by her sincerity and with tear-filled eyes I slowly removed the cover. But I burst into laughter as my eyes fixed on a stuffed-animal piggy with a piece of green broccoli poking out of its mouth. The pig wore a sign saying, "You've saved my life too! Thank you!"

Seventeen years have passed and Kathy is still alive and appreciating every day of her life. She continues to be a good friend. Surprisingly, she maintains the same diet I gave her long ago. Since her recovery, she's spent extensive time researching vegetarianism, and thanks to her I am also more informed about the topic. Much of this book includes information we've shared as our paths of healing have unfolded.

Increasingly, scientists, physicians, and health practitioners agree that eating less or no meat is better for our health. Today there are numerous options for combining grains, legumes, vegetables, and fruits to provide complete protein and all the nutrients we require.

The belief that meat provides our bodies with more strength is debunked by studies showing that vegetarians eating a balanced diet have at least as much strength and endurance as meat eaters. Think of how much hard work a horse or ox can do and realize that all that energy is obtained from grasses and grains!

In terms of the most efficient and productive use of land to grow and supply the world with protein foods, we find that one acre of earth can produce up to twenty times as much consumable protein in the form of grains or legumes as in the form of meat products. It is more economical, humane, and environmentally sound to eat a vegetarian diet.

Just like humans, animals suffer from many diseases. And like humans, they process and eliminate bodily toxins and wastes through their organs, especially their kidneys. When an animal dies, its kidneys and all other organs cease to function; toxins are trapped in the body and seep into the muscular flesh. This is what a meat eater will consume.

At the time of slaughter, animals can be in a state of panic. As an automatic defense mechanism, their bodies produce and secrete an abundant amount of adrenaline. Adrenaline is a hormone that speeds up the heart rate and raises blood pressure and blood sugar in order to help animals cope with stress. Under normal circumstances, after a crisis has passed, the kidneys eliminate excess adrenaline through the urine. However, upon death, the animal's body cannot eliminate the hormone and the adrenaline passes into the muscles. Because of this stored adrenaline in meat, eating meat in large amounts can lead to increased heart rate, high blood pressure, unbalanced blood sugar levels, and other related debilities. Evidence indicates that, in general, vegetarians have less heart disease and fewer blood sugar problems than meat eaters. They also expend less energy eliminating toxins from their bodies.

Articles in major newspapers and magazines report that the greatest hidden danger to the health of meat eaters is the amount of potentially harmful invisible pollutants in meat, including bacteria, pesticides, preservatives, hormones, antibiotics, and other chemical remnants. While bacteria come from low quality standards in butchering and processing, the other chemicals are used during the production process. By eliminating meat from our diets, we cut out a source of many potentially harmful or disease-related chemicals.

Myths about Vegetarianism

NEED FOR SUPPLEMENTS

I'm often asked, "Do I need to take vitamin supplements if I'm a vegetarian?" Whether we are vegetarians or meat eaters, these days vitamin supplements are almost always necessary. However, many people have gone from taking no vitamins to swallowing inappropriate megadoses of all kinds of vitamins.

The use of vitamin supplements should not be tailored to what is trendy or what other people do. In general, anyone who is able to follow a consistently wholesome and well-planned diet does not need a lot of vitamin supplements. Unfortunately, we are living in such a fast-paced and stressful world that many of us do not consume the balanced variety of vitamins and minerals we need. Too often, it's only after we suffer loss of health and well-being in ourselves or our loved ones that we begin to seriously look into balanced nutrition and preventive or healing measures.

Moderate use of vitamin supplements is encouraged, but it is not wise to take vitamins in order to compensate for poor and erratic dietary habits. Sometimes, taking megadoses of vitamins causes more distress in the system. Vitamin overdoses tend to raise yang energy, causing the depletion of yin energy and unbalancing our metabolism. Symptoms such as skin rash, red eyes, headache, constipation or diarrhea, acne, acidic stomach, burping, short temper, and metallic taste in the mouth can be indications of an overdose of vitamins.

However, vitamin supplements in moderate amounts are often necessary to nourish and strengthen the body. They help us recover from illness or surgery more quickly. Vitamins used correctly can nourish tissue cells, improve metabolic function, and improve the capacity to resist disease immunologically.

Herbal supplements are vastly complex and require extensive study. In this small book, I can only provide some information about a few helpful vitamin and herb tonics. Among the thousands of powerful herbs, you will find that *Panax quinquefolium, Angelica sinensis, Lycium chinesis,* and *Ganoderma lucidum* are a few that are useful as qi and blood tonics. Vitamin E (d-alphatocopherol), wheat germ oil, or lecithin is often added to the formulas to enhance their functioning.

- PANAX QUINQUEFOLIUM is known in the West as ginseng. Western ginseng grows in Korea, Japan, the United States, and Canada. Ginseng can be used to eliminate internal heat; it is a qi tonic that increases and strengthens the body's vital energy, relieves fatigue, and stimulates blood circulation.

- ANGELICA SINENSIS is grown largely in China and Japan. The common name for this blood tonic herb is tang-kwei. Tang-kwei contains essential oil, palmatic acid, and vitamin B complex. Tang-kwei improves blood circulation and helps treat anemia, constipation, irregular menstruation, and injury trauma.

- LYCIUM CHINESIS can reduce fever. It invigorates the liver and kidneys, increases the essential energy of the blood, strengthens the tendons and bones, and as a result, nourishes the blood. Its essential oils exert a diuretic effect.

- GANODERMA LUCIDUM is commonly called Reishi mushroom. The Chinese recognize it as the "herb of good fortune." Reishi mushroom has long been used in Oriental medicine as a life-prolonging herb. It is known to enhance immunity. Recently, pharmaceutical companies have been doing extensive studies of Reishi and its beneficial effects in treating bronchitis, hepatitis, arthritis, neurasthenia, and hypertension.

- VITAMIN E is thought to retard cellular aging and keep skin younger looking. It can alleviate fatigue, improve endurance, prevent blood clots, and prevent thick scar formation externally and internally. Vitamin E deficiency is related to anemia, muscle degeneration, and destruction of red blood cells. Wheat germ oil is a good source of Vitamin E.

- LECITHIN is usually added to enhance the functioning of Vitamin E; it assists in transporting fatty cells and cholesterol from the blood. It is important in preventing arteriosclerosis.

VITAMIN B12 DEFICIENCY

Vitamin B12 is essential for proper development and health of the central nervous system. Nowadays, there are many new sources of B12 being introduced and B12 deficiency is no longer a threat to vegetarians. B12 can be found in tempeh (products made from soybeans and grains), sea vegetables, and many fortified soy products.

Michio Kushi, a macrobiotic expert, suggests 5 milligrams per day of B12 for adults, and he recommends sea vegetables, tempeh, and miso as sources of this essential nutrient. Nori (a seaweed) is very high in B12, having about 13 milligrams of B12 in each 100 grams of its dried form. Other sea vegetables yield about 6 milligrams per 100 grams of their dried form.

LACK OF CALCIUM

Calcium deficiency is sometimes a concern for vegetarians because calcium is not as readily available in plant foods as in animal foods. In my clinical experience, I've found that calcium deficiency may not be due to inadequate calcium intake but rather to lack of absorption due to improper amounts of phosphorous in the diet. Fast foods, processed products, soft drinks, refined sugar, caffeine, and stress increase acidity in the body and also interfere with calcium absorption.

Sea vegetables are good sources of calcium and also supply iodine, iron, vitamins A, B, C, E, and protein. Seaweeds at your local health food store include agar-agar, arame, dulse, hiijiki, kelp, kombu, nori, and wakame. Sea vegetables are very versatile. They can be shredded over any grain dish, cooked with other vegetables, added to stir-fry dishes, used in making soup stock, or sprinkled on top of your favorite salad dishes. Nori is a popular wrapper for sushi.

OTHER GOOD SOURCES OF CALCIUM ARE:

Toasted whole sesame seed: 281 milligrams calcium/ounce

Toasted hulled sesame seed: 37 milligrams calcium/ounce

Broccoli: 188 milligrams calcium/cup

Pinto beans: 89 milligrams calcium/cup

Tahini: 64 milligrams calcium/tablespoon

Good sources of phosphorous (needed for absorption of calcium) are whole grain breads, cereals, and nuts.

SUFFICIENT CARBOHYDRATES

Our best sources of energy are carbohydrates, which can be found in fruits, grains, and vegetables. Sugars are simple carbohydrates, while starches are termed complex carbohydrates. Starches (such as those in potatoes, wheat, rice, corn, carrots, and turnips, for example) support a more consistent blood sugar level while sugars (fruit sugar, milk sugar, cane sugar, and so on) can cause rapid fluctuation in blood glucose levels. A well-rounded vegetarian diet will automatically provide plenty of carbohydrates to consistently fuel our energy all day long. Some carbohydrates should constitute at least fifty percent of our diet; healthy vegetarianism is an ideal way to ensure this.

The Vegetarian Diet

A true vegetarian (also known as a vegan) eats only grains, fruits, legumes, vegetables, and other plant matter; all animal and dairy products are avoided. Other forms of vegetarianism include eating milk products but not eggs (lacto-vegetarianism) and eating both milk and egg products (lacto-ova-vegetarianism).

Vegetarians need to be particularly concerned about consuming adequate protein; in this regard, soybeans are one of the primary protein sources. Soybeans and soy-based products, including tofu, tempeh, and soy milk, offer complete protein in the form of all the essential amino acids in the proper proportions to promote growth and development.

Some other high-quality protein foods are wheat germ, chick peas (garbanzo beans), sunflower seeds, sesame seeds, and some nuts. However, these foods do not contain all the essential amino acids; they need to be consumed with other foods that furnish the missing amino acids. For example, combining sesame seeds with brown rice provides complete protein.

Vegetables with some protein value include green beans, broccoli, mustard greens, artichokes, potatoes, pumpkins, and squashes. Grains, seeds, and nuts contain some amino acids but are low in others.

You can see that a diet providing plenty of protein is attainable without eating meat. However, a plate of salad and vegetables is not considered an adequate meal. Adding some tofu or brown rice and sesame seeds will fulfill the requirements for a complete healthy meal. Your diet and cooking need not be complex to satisfy nutritional requirements as well as your palate.

There is such a diversity of tastes and textures among soy products, grains, legumes, vegetables, seeds, nuts, and fruits that you need never get bored. In fact, the more you explore, the greater your interest and knowledge will grow. With grains alone, you can try buckwheat, blue corn, quinoa, amaranth, and teff to supplement the more common rice, wheat, oats, and rye. Teff is an especially wholesome grain that provides abundant amounts of protein—up to 172 milligrams per 100-gram serving, which compares to oats' 55 milligrams or hard winter wheat's 46 milligrams per 100-gram serving. Teff also provides two to three times the iron found in wheat or barley. Take advantage of this wonderful, highly nutritious food by eating white teff for protein and red teff for iron; teff is also a great substitute food for those who are allergic to wheat.

The following list suggests specific foods as sources for some of our basic nutritional requirements.

- HIGHER PROTEINS: Asparagus, barley, black-eyed peas, broccoli, brown rice, brussels sprouts, buckwheat, bulgur wheat, cauliflower, corn on the cob, cornmeal, garbanzo beans, green beans, green peas, kidney beans, lima beans, millet, navy beans, northern beans, oats, okra, peanuts, rye, soybeans, spinach, whole wheat

- MODERATE PROTEINS: Beet greens, collard greens, kale, mustard greens, potatoes, sweet potatoes, swiss chard, winter squash, yams

- VITAMIN A: Apricots, asparagus, avocados, beets, broccoli, brussels sprouts, cantaloupe, carrots, cherries, chinese cabbage, collard greens, eggplant, endives, lettuce (leaf), mangoes, mustard seed, nectarines, peaches, peas, plantains, pumpkins, red peppers, spinach, squash, sweet potatoes, tomatoes, turnip greens

- B VITAMINS: Avocados, black-eyed peas, brewer's yeast, green peas, jerusalem artichokes, lettuce (leaf), oranges, pineapples, raisins, tomatoes, watermelon

- VITAMIN C: Broccoli, brussels sprouts, cantaloupe, cauliflower, grapefruit, lemons, oranges, peaches, red peppers, strawberries

- CALCIUM: Almonds, beans, beet greens, broccoli, chinese cabbage, collard greens, eggplant, figs, kale, oranges, sesame seeds, soybeans, teff, turnip greens

- COPPER: Almonds, apricots, avocados, broccoli, brazil nuts, currants, figs, hazelnuts, kidney beans, lima beans, mushrooms, navy beans, peas, peanuts, pecans, prunes, walnuts

Making the Transition

Even if you have committed yourself to vegetarian eating, it may not always be easy to incorporate it into your lifestyle. At the beginning you might feel confused about changes you notice in yourself; you might wonder how to maintain vegetarian eating in unusual circumstances, and you might be unsure about some of the foods and how to prepare them. This section addresses some of these concerns.

YIN/YANG

Whether we choose to be vegetarian or not, the balance of yin/yang and acid/alkaline in food preparation and intake is vital. As a rule of thumb, it is advisable to have one part yin (acidic) food to five parts yang (alkaline) food. This way the body will be less susceptible to acid-prone symptoms and a more healthy alkaline state can be maintained. The following list of sample yin and yang foods will help you decide how to balance your cooking.

Some Yin Foods

Vegetables: artichokes, bamboo shoots, beets, carrots, cucumbers, eggplants, green beans, mushrooms, radishes, spinach, summer squash, sweet potatoes, tomatoes, yams, zucchini

Fruits: avocados, bananas, grapefruit, lemons, limes, mangoes, melons, oranges, papayas, persimmons, pineapples, tamarinds, tangerines

Legumes: mung beans, peanuts

Grains: pearly barley, sweet rice

Seasonings: black pepper, ginger, parsley

Sweeteners: honey, molasses, syrups

Dairy: butter, cheese, ice cream, milk, yogurt

Miscellaneous: caffeine (chocolate, coffee, cola, hot or iced tea), soft drinks, vinegar

Some Yang Foods

Vegetables: lettuce, turnips, winter squash

Fruits: apples, cherries, winter melons

Legumes: aduki beans, black beans, kidney beans, navy beans

Grains: brown rice, white rice, flour

Seasonings: cinnamon, coriander, real salt, soy sauce, olive oil, peanut oil, sesame oil, soybean oil

Miscellaneous: lotus leaf tea, lotus seeds, lotus roots, ginseng

SUBSTITUTE FOODS

As the following list demonstrates, it's not difficult to substitute vegetarian products for things that may not be as good for us. All the substitutes listed can be found at health food stores, oriental groceries, or your local supermarket.

TRADITIONAL FOOD	SUBSTITUTE FOOD
animal protein	tofu, tempeh, seitan, TVP (texturized vegetable protein)
bacon	bacon-flavored crunch soy bits
butter	canola margarine, nut butters
candy	carob bars, granola bars
cheese	soy cheese, almond cheese
coffee	chicory, pearl barley grain coffee
commercially grown vegetables	organically grown vegetables
cottage cheese	cottage tofu
crackers	rice cakes
ground beef	texturized vegetable protein (TVP)
ice cream	rice cream
mayonnaise	vegenaise
meat broth	vegetable broth
milk (cow's, goat's)	soy milk, rice milk, oat milk
potato chips	baked potato chips, carrot chips
processed oil	cold pressed oil
refined salt	real salt
onion	marinated cabbage
pizza (cheese and meat)	vegetable and soy pizza
sausage	soy links
scrambled eggs	tofu scramble
seafood	mock seafood (made from bean curd, seaweed, taro powder)
soft drinks	carbonated spring water
sugar	stevia, Sucanat®, raw sugar
tap or well water	filtered purified water or certified natural spring water
waxed, sprayed fruit	organically grown fruit
white bread	whole grain bread

BODY AND MIND

To feel confident you are consuming ample protein, vitamins, minerals, and enzymes to provide your body with all the fuel and nutrients it needs, it is important to eat a wide range of grains, legumes, vegetables, seeds, nuts, and fruits. Exploring the recipes in this book will aid you in preparing wholesome, nutritious meals. There are many other books available that detail the amounts of nutrients found in vegetarian foods and how to combine foods for complementary protein and complete nutrition.

Give yourself time to get accustomed to the tastes of new foods. At first, the good taste of a food may elude you simply because your taste buds aren't used to it. As you try more vegetarian foods and methods of preparing them, you'll discover many new tastes and textures that will be very pleasing and satisfying. Something that may have tasted bland in the beginning, due perhaps to previously overstimulated taste buds, often becomes a favorite food as you learn to enjoy its subtleties.

Be especially careful in observing how your mind is working. Your mind can provide lots of positive reinforcement and reminders about why eating vegetarian foods is important; it can also constantly sidetrack you and give you lots of reasons to give up.

In the process of learning to eat a vegetarian diet, be mindful of the following points:

- Make the transition gradually as you eliminate animal foods from your diet. At first, you might want to try vegetarian meals only a few days a week. Try not to make the transition while you're going through an emotional crisis or other major lifestyle change. If you want to begin by committing only a few days a month, you can purchase a Chinese lunar calendar at an oriental grocery store and use it to eat vegetarian meals on the most important days of the month, as follows:

DAYS COMMITTED	MOST IMPORTANT DATES OF MONTH
2 days	1st and 15th (full moon and new moon)
4 days	1st, 8th, 15th, and 23rd
6 days	1st, 8th, 14th, 15th, 23rd, and last day
10 days	1st, 8th, 14th, 15th, 18th, 23rd, 24th, 28th, and last day

- As you progress, you may want to commit to a month of vegetarian eating to help purify and cleanse your body. Eventually you may find you prefer eating vegetarian all the time.

- Eating meat over a long period of time can be addictive, and any long-term habit or addiction can be difficult to break. Based on this knowledge, don't be hard on yourself or quickly give up if you stumble in your attempt to become a vegetarian. It may take a number of tries before you totally give up meat.

- When you change your diet you may feel tired or weak. This is not necessarily reason for concern as long as you are generally healthy and you are getting all the nutrients you need in proper quantity. Your body is probably releasing toxins that have been stored from your meat-eating days. It is detoxing and the reaction is similar to stopping alcohol or cigarettes. Record your daily activities and all the foods you are eating. When you examine this record, you may discover your diet isn't balanced or perhaps something in your activities is tiring you. Any fatigue or weakness you feel from detoxing should be better within a week or so.

- Commitment and perseverance are required for attaining any worthy goal. Be patient and don't feel guilty if you falter; use your mind for positive reinforcement—it can be a powerful tool and ally. Remember, you can control your mind, it need not control you.

- If after many trials you are unable to let go of your desire for meat, don't be disappointed. This may not be the time to become vegetarian; chances are you will fulfill your goal at a later date.

EATING ON THE ROAD

Patients often ask me, "How can I maintain my healthy vegetarian regime while I'm on the road?" While this does take some effort, it is not terribly difficult. Several years ago, one of my patients was an ambassador to one of the European countries; he traveled often and his schedule was hectic. Each time he returned to the United States, he and his wife would come to see me for treatments. His wife told me that even though her husband was frequently traveling while abroad and usually had back-to-back meetings, he always insisted on bringing his own food wherever he went. "He follows the diet you gave him to a T," she proudly reported.

Here are some hints to help you follow a vegetarian plan when you're away from home.

- Make a mental commitment to continue your eating style while on your trip. Don't allow yourself to slip up or you may feel sorry afterward.

- Adjust your meals to whatever time zone you're in and eat accordingly; don't think about what time it is at home.

- Bring plenty of non-carbonated mineral water to drink (if it's not available where you're going), and avoid soft drinks, cold drinks, and acidic fruit juices. A glass of body-temperature mineral water with a twist of lemon or lime is always refreshing and lessens stressful effects of travel.

- It might help to eat smaller meals and increase your intake of carbohydrates like potatoes, rice, and grains.

- Plan ahead and try to pack whatever foods you need that might not be available while you travel. Most airlines will accommodate a request for a vegetarian meal, but often these meals don't provide the nutrients needed during the stresses of travel. It's simple to pack a few snacks for the plane; an almond butter sandwich on whole grain bread or celery sticks with tahini can be used to supplement airline food.

STAYING WITH FRIENDS AND RELATIVES

Let your hosts know in advance about your dietary requirements, not that they should purchase special foods for you, but simply out of courtesy. Explain to them that vegetarianism means no meat or animal products whatsoever, including meat broths or other foods cooked with meat. If your hosts offer to buy food for you, tell them exactly what you eat so that they do not stock up on inappropriate items only to learn you can't eat them. I once arrived as guest of honor at a table set for a feast; however, the casserole contained meat, and when I informed my hostess that I was a vegetarian, she replied, "I know what to do, I'll pull the meat out of your portion." Tactfully do whatever you can to let your hosts know ahead of time about your eating habits.

Eat simply; don't expect elaborate meals. If time is a factor, you can eat only two meals a day—a large breakfast and an early supper. Don't allow yourself to splurge with the thought that you'll return to good eating when you get home. You'll pay for this with depleted energy: travel is stressful and takes more energy than your normal routine. Don't cheat yourself by slipping out of your vegetarian diet and having less energy to enjoy yourself or carry out your business. If you don't eat your healthy vegetarian cuisine while away from home, you may return feeling weak or sick.

HOTEL ACCOMMODATIONS

If possible, plan your hotel or motel stay to include a room with a kitchenette. Even if it costs a little more, you will easily make up that cost by preparing your own food instead of going out to eat all the time. You'll be well nourished and have peace of mind knowing that your dietary requirements are being met. If you cannot find a kitchenette, here are a few other ideas:

• Look for an oriental restaurant. You can always order tofu, rice, and vegetables there, and you can request your meal be prepared with no MSG, onions, or garlic (see the information on pungent spices in the next chapter).

• Italian restaurants will usually have at least one vegetarian dish such as a no-meat lasagna or spaghetti with meatless sauce.

• Indian restaurants also have a number of vegetarian selections.

• Check the yellow pages for listings of vegetarian restaurants.

• Health food stores sometimes have carry-out prepared vege-tarian foods. At a minimum, they will have prepackaged prod-ucts such as granola, soy milk, tempeh, and so on.

Whether you travel near or far, keep in mind that life is pre-cious and you can't take a vacation from taking care of yourself. If you're not pursuing your optimum health, you are limiting yourself, whether you're at home or far away. The present moment is always the moment you have to work with in your pursuit—use it well whether you're working, relaxing, or travel-ing for business or pleasure. In this way, a successful trip is always at hand. Bon voyage!

Important Elements
of Good Health

PERSONAL ENVIRONMENT

The benefits of eating well are complemented by improving your personal living and working space. If you read the labels on household, hygiene, and beauty products, you may find many potentially unhealthy substances are surrounding you. Numerous chemicals commonly used in our living environments have been linked to allergies, low energy levels, headaches, and mental fatigue. In your health food store and increasingly in grocery stores, you can find household and cosmetic products without toxic chemicals. There are also a number of independent distributors of such products. A good-quality air purifier can help reduce the number of atmospheric pollutants in your home or office.

WATER

Our bodies are comprised mostly of water, and while we can survive several days or weeks without food, we can only last three or four days without water. Thus, water for drinking, cooking, bathing, and washing is an extremely important factor in our effort to be well.

Today, our drinking-water sources are bombarded with many pollutants. Bacteria, chlorine, fluoride, lead, and other heavy metals and chemicals abound in our water supplies. It's a good idea to have your tap water tested; if toxins are evident, consider investing in a good-quality water purifier. Reverse-osmosis systems are generally accepted as the most thorough purifying method. If you purchase a portable unit, I recommend it include a silver-impregnated strong acid calton resin (SCR), silver-impregnated granular activated carbon (GAC), and filter fabric. Silver prevents bacteria buildup inside the cartridge.

Bottled water is an alternative to buying a purifier, but be careful. Many bottled waters are as polluted as your tap water. You can have a test run on the bottled water or demand certification that the water is free of harmful chemicals or pollutants.

ORGANIC PRODUCE

Modern agriculture is designed for efficiency and profit. Too often, little concern is given to the nutritional value of the food. The result is vegetables and fruits heavily contaminated by chemical fertilizers and pesticides. Grocery stores often stock their shelves with produce containing a lot of toxins.

Fortunately, there is a growing movement toward sustainable agriculture and organic foods. This method of farming can provide us with nutritious foods safe for consumption while nourishing and sustaining the soil. Health food stores stock organic produce, and if you have the time, nothing can compare with the satisfaction and taste of growing your own organic foods.

PUNGENT SPICES

I recommend little or no use of what are called the five turbid plants: onion, garlic, chives, leeks, and shallots. As we've learned more about the effects of these plants over the years, we've come to realize that they can cause overheating of the body and the emotions. Body odor also lessens when we decrease our intake of the turbid plants.

Instead, use ginger, lemongrass, cumin, turmeric, coriander, oregano, thyme, bay leaves, or other seasonings. Occasionally we may need to make an exception in order to use one of the pungent plants as part of a cure for an illness, but regular use of these plants is strongly discouraged.

Frequency of Meals

Three balanced meals a day are highly recommended, especially if your lifestyle is busy and stressful. If you don't enjoy spending time in the kitchen, cook extra food at lunch and eat half at lunch and the other half at dinner.

However, it's not a good idea to frequently keep leftovers overnight. Food loses its vitality and nutritional value if it sits overnight in the refrigerator. Habitually eating leftovers can make you feel fatigued.

Some other things to keep in mind about timing of meals are:

- Eat dinner early in the evening; otherwise you won't have time to properly digest your food before going to bed. Lying down with a full stomach or while you're still actively digesting may allow stomach acid to reflux into your esophagus and cause belching and acid indigestion. You should be up for at least three hours after you eat dinner; eating before six p.m. is helpful for weight-watchers.

- Early morning is when your stomach is most active and the time when you need fuel to start your long day of activities. Just as it's wise to fuel up your car for a long trip, so you should fuel your body each morning.

- Your body slows down in late afternoon and begins the process of waste disposal and purification that continues while you sleep. Eating late disrupts this natural cleaning process.

Taking Care of Yourself

In our efforts to eat well and feel better, we will certainly encounter times of sickness or fatigue. In working with my patients over the years, I've found it remarkable that although we accumulate all kinds of knowledge through our educational systems and life experiences, very little of it has to do with healing our own bodies or those of our loved ones.

This section offers some principles of self care for body and mind. If your mind is at ease, your body will respond more quickly to healing techniques. Although I discuss only a few ailments in this book, the principles presented can be used in a commonsense way and applied to a variety of symptoms.

ASTHMA AND ALLERGIES

Chronic asthma or allergies can cause respiratory difficulties. The body becomes congested with mucus and built-up toxins. Often, the bowel becomes stagnated, causing the lungs to try to eliminate more toxins. Thus, the lungs become irritated along with the mucous membranes. Asthma has a strong emotional component which cannot be addressed by inhalers and drugs. Some tips for dealing with asthma and allergies follow.

- Eat plenty of green leafy vegetables and whole grains

- Eliminate alcohol, cigarettes, coffee, and spicy foods

- Drink purified water instead of soft drinks

- Stay away from areas where heavy chemicals are in use

- A bowel-cleansing program can be helpful

- Use an air purifier

- Exercises such as tai chi or yoga are recommended

- Practice breathing exercises and learn to breath properly

- Follow a less hectic schedule and create a peaceful environment

- Address any underlying emotional causes

- Learn to meditate and practice daily

BODILY ACHES AND PAINS

Lifestyle and emotional conditions often underlie aches and pains in our backs, necks, shoulders, hips, and other joints and muscles. Regardless of medication or surgery (both of which can be harmful), our bodily aches may continue until we change lifestyle or eating habits and focus on fulfilling a higher purpose in this life. Some hints for dealing with body aches are:

- Follow a diet rich in carbohydrates, green leafy vegetables, and soy protein

- Use polyunsaturated oils instead of saturated fat

- Avoid alcohol, cigarettes, and coffee

- Exercise regularly

- Make lists of priorities and try to live a simpler life

- Eat regular meals

- Avoid overexposure to televisions, microwaves, computers, and fluorescent lights

- Deal with emotional problems that are bothering you but you refuse to talk about

- Be moderate in your sexual activities

CANCER

The causes of cancer are so many and varied that I cannot present a list of do's and don'ts for this illness. In treating my patients, I emphasize that significant changes in lifestyle and attitude are necessary in the cure for cancer. Major sickness is sometimes necessary in order to encourage people to take a careful look at their lives. For seriously ill patients, a quick cure can be more dangerous than the disease itself because the patient may not have learned to change what caused the cancer.

Any illness can be the means to urge us to reexamine our lives and discover our true nature. Sickness can alert us to our ignorance and arrogance and show us we've lost track of what is truly important. It has been well said that "All sickness is homesickness." All forms of illness are an alert that we have lost touch with something significant; disease can be a means for rediscovering what life is all about. In this way, sickness can transform your life for the better.

Studies have shown that a healthy diet can be important in preventing cancer and is helpful in the cure. Folic acid, a B vitamin, can help repair DNA, which is the cell's central control mechanism causing normal cells to become cancer cells. Some sources of folic acid are:

- asparagus
- black beans

- kidney beans
- lentils

- black-eyed peas
- broccoli
- brussels sprouts
- garbanzo beans (chick peas)
- great northern beans
- lima beans
- navy beans
- pinto beans
- soybeans
- spinach

However, anybody with cancer needs to examine all aspects of their life, including diet, job, relationships, exercise, personal environments, and emotional or mental problems. Patients should work closely with a holistic healer who exhibits compassion as well as medical knowledge and whose own life is a role model for the patient.

COLDS AND FLU

Although we often think of colds and flu as minor illnesses, it is also true that they are the forerunners or first symptoms of many major diseases. It's best to take good care of these common ailments before they manifest in deeper levels of your body. The following suggestions should help you.

- Eat small meals frequently; a bowl of soup with a piece of toast and glass of natural ginger ale is good

- Drink plenty of purified water, lemonade, or warm tea

- Drink ginger tea as long as there is no fever present

- Don't eat rice until your symptoms are completely gone; eat whole wheat noodles instead

- Get lots of rest

- Avoid over-covering the body if you have a fever; applying lemon or lime slices to the temples, forehead, armpits, and groin will help reduce your temperature

- Stay away from noise, television, the computer, excessive reading, long conversations, and emotional conflicts

- Soothe yourself with peaceful music

- Stay out of drafts and winds

- Sexual activity will prolong illness

- Don't take baths or showers; a dry bath is advisable until you are well

- Do take an herbal steam; the sweat will open your pores and help release toxins from the lymph nodes

- Drink some warm rice milk or lemonade following the herbal steam to quench any dryness and soothe your body

- After your herbal steam, put on warm clothes; go to bed, and cover yourself with a cotton blanket. Rest for 45 minutes or longer

- Don't feel victimized by your illness; appreciate that you're alive

DIABETES

Diabetes is a form of cell starvation. When the body's insulin, a hormone, is not working properly, cells do not receive enough of the simple sugar called glucose. Instead, sugar builds up in the blood and the cells don't get enough for the proper functioning of their microscopic machinery. The excess sugar in the blood is excreted by way of the urine. Symptoms of diabetes can include excessive urination, thirst, dehydration, weight loss, and weakness. The condition can be serious if not treated and can lead to labored breathing and coma. A couple of important dietary requirements for diabetes are:

- Include plenty of complex carbohydrates and fiber to ensure more gradual release of sugars into the bloodstream

- Fats and oils should be used in moderation because they interfere with the functioning of insulin

DIARRHEA

Diarrhea, not properly taken care of, can lead to serious health problems. If it persists for a couple of days or is a recurring condition, consult a holistic health practitioner for a thorough diagnosis.

- Don't eat fruit or raw vegetables

- Don't eat fatty or deep-fried foods

- Drink carbonated water and eat some crackers

- Eat roasted rice soup (see "Rice and Noodles" recipe section)

- Keep the abdomen warm and away from drafts

- Don't expose yourself to wind and cold

And remember, sickness can be a result of the way we conduct our lives. Although diet is critical, the state of our mind and general lifestyle are essential to any healing, Recovering from sickness is not really our ultimate goal; rather, we want to learn more about ourselves and our potential to appreciate each moment of life. Our illnesses can actually be a means to increased happiness and well-being.

Tea and Your Health

For hundreds of years, tea has been second only to water as the favored beverage in Asia. Tea is prized for its ability to banish fatigue and stimulate mental power. It enhances lightness of spirit and clarity of mind while relieving feelings of mental or physical constriction. When we sit down with a cup of tea, we feel more serene and the agitations of daily life are put to rest for a while.

There is a Chinese proverb that translated literally could read:

> Drinking a daily cup of tea
> Will surely starve the apothecary.

Or, to give it a more American spin:

> A daily cup of tea or more
> Keeps you out of the drugstore.

TYPES OF TEA

There are two kinds of caffeinated teas, black and green. They both come from the same plant; the difference lies in processing.

Black tea goes through the longest oxidation, or fermentation, process. Oolong tea is oxidized about half as long as black tea. Leaves for oolong tea must be picked just when they reach their peak and not left to wither; then they are processed immediately. Oolong is the tea most often served in Chinese restaurants.

Green tea is not oxidized. Instead the leaves are processed by microorganisms and the leaves may nor may not be withered. They are de-enzymed by pan frying, then the leaves are rolled and fired and they turn a yellow-green. The five best known Chinese green teas are: Lung Ching, Huangshan Mao Feng, Pi Lo Chun, Puto Fo Cha, and Lu'an Guapian.

When you pour boiling water over tea leaves, you release the useful ingredients of caffeine, aromatic or essential oils, and polyphenol (tannin).

CAFFEINE

Caffeine stimulates the intestinal tract and increases the flow of digestive juices. This could be one reason a cup of tea after a greasy meal helps alleviate feelings of discomfort. In moderate amounts, caffeine stimulates the process of elimination, promotes circulation, and acts as a diuretic, promoting better kidney function.

Despite numerous studies of caffeine, no direct links have been shown between moderate intake of this chemical and serious illness. And there is some evidence that tea drinkers have a lower incidence of kidney ailments and gallstones. For comparison purposes, there are about 30 milligrams of caffeine in a cup of green tea, about 40 in oolong tea, and about 50 in a cup of black tea. This compares to about 150 milligrams of caffeine in a cup of drip coffee.

ESSENTIAL OILS

Sometimes called aromatic oils and sometimes volatile (because they completely evaporate), essential oils develop in tea leaves as they grow. These substances aid digestion and help emulsify fat. Green tea has more essential oil than the more highly processed black tea.

POLYPHENOLS

These substances may act as anti-cancer agents. They help DNA reproduce correctly rather than in a mutated form. Polyphenols can also increase white blood cells, the soldiers that fight infection in the body. For these reasons, in China the drinking of certain teas is part of the treatment for nephritis, chronic hepatitis, and leukemia.

TEA AND CANCER

Researchers at the Chinese Academy of Preventive Medicine have found that drinking tea can inhibit the action or formation of cancer-causing substances. For example, tea may block the action of nitrosamine, which has been linked to cancer. Green tea has the highest blocking action, with other teas having less blocking ability. One gram of tea has some effect, but three to five grams (three grams is a teaspoonful) have a much stronger effect.

Studies conducted at a university in China link lower rates of stomach and liver cancer with geographic areas in Japan and China where the population consumes large quantities of strong tea, especially green tea. Mortality rates from these diseases were lower in places where strong tea was imbibed frequently.

TEA AND YOUR HEART

Recent studies have also shown that tea may have an advantageous effect on your heart. It may work in a general way to help prevent heart disease and strokes by:

- gently stimulating the heart and circulatory system

- strengthening and toning the blood vessels

- decreasing cholesterol through its phenol content (especially oolong tea)

- decreasing the blood's tendency to form thrombi, or unwanted clots

Claims have been made that tea actually reduces the amount of fat in the tissues; oolong tea has received the most attention regarding this. Tea may even contribute to longevity by improving stomach function and reducing the chance of heart disease. The fluoride content in tea can help strengthen bones and dental enamel.

NUTRIENTS IN TEA

Tea contains vitamins B1, B2, K, P, niacin, folic acid, and manganese. A cup of black tea has 58 milligrams of potassium, and green tea is a source of vitamin C. With the increasing popularity of tea drinking, a variety of teas are now available in grocery stores, health food stores, and oriental groceries.

HOW TO MAKE A FINE CUP OF TEA

Tea preparation is an art requiring little time and bestowing many benefits. To start, make sure you have fresh spring water to enhance the taste of the tea. Each cup of water requires one teaspoon of loose tea or one tea bag; for more than six cups, add an extra spoonful or tea bag "for the pot."

First, heat a little more water than you need for the amount of tea you're making. When the water is hot, use some of it to rinse and heat the teapot and the cups. Just before the rest of the water boils, empty the teapot and add the tea. Pour the boiled water over it and let the tea stand no longer than five minutes. About three-fourths of the caffeine is released after five minutes of infusion. For stronger tea, use more leaves, not more time. Black tea colors quickly, but green tea should never get dark.

Never use milk with green tea; if you use it with black or oolong tea, add the milk to the cup first. Don't use cream with tea because the tannin in tea will cause the cream to curdle.

Before pouring tea, stir it or shake the pot and let the leaves settle. Empty the hot rinse water out of the cups, and pour the tea through a strainer if it's loose tea. If you use lemon and sugar, put the sugar in before pouring the tea so that it can dissolve well. Stevia can be substituted for sugar for a pleasant taste. Adding lemon, which contains the enzyme tannase, may help the body absorb nutrients from the tea.

Oolong and black tea hold up well through a second infusion—in fact, many people say the second infusion is the best. However, don't reuse tea that has stood overnight; it may actually have harmful effects. Finally, to make iced tea, use about fifty percent more tea to allow for the diluting effects of melting ice.

Take the time to prepare, sip, and enjoy your tea as a replenishing break during your day. You'll feel relaxed and renewed from this simple effort.

A New Attitude about Food

When planning your meals, consider the whole meal and not just the data behind the foods (calories, fat content, amount of protein, and so on). If you keep your sights on a well-rounded intake consisting primarily of grains, legumes, vegetables, and small portions of fruits, you don't need to dissect the contents of each and every meal.

If you are constantly worried about what you're eating, your mind will bring tension instead of creativity to your meals, and your body will neither digest well nor enjoy the food you're preparing. In our diet and lifestyle, we're seeking integration, not fragmentation. We want to increase our awareness and be flexible in using our intuition and imagination as we place emphasis on healing through nutrition.

Nutrition is a major part of my medical practice, and many times my patients expect to receive a handful of papers filled with facts when I begin to discuss diet with them. They're surprised when, instead, I ask them to carefully record everything they eat for a week. Once I have this report in hand, we evaluate their diet in relation to their health, and I begin to guide them in what to eat. Often, a look of apprehension appears and I see them thinking, "I can't do that."

However, as the consultation progresses and I walk them through the process, they begin to realize that a balanced diet is not as complicated as they thought. Most of the foods I prescribe are not uncommon, and as my patients learn how to prepare these foods, I can see creativity and excitement replace fear and anxiety about eating in a new way.

Each week, my clients fill out another diet report, and as they realize my commitment to their nutrition and become committed to it themselves, I notice they are no longer anxious about reporting their eating habits. There is mutual satisfaction in sharing a major life transition as I support people in taking responsibility for their own healing. My patients appreciate having a good coach, and I hope the knowledge in this book will help coach and support you in healthy vegetarian eating.

FOODS IN THE VEGETARIAN DIET

If you're just beginning to prepare vegetarian meals, the following information on some vegetarian foods may be helpful. I've found that it's wise to begin simply in preparing your vegetarian meals, then slowly add more diversity as you get increasingly comfortable with a variety of foods. Many vegetarian items can be purchased at your grocery stores; try a health food store or oriental grocery if you can't find something at the supermarket.

Amazake

Made from cultured whole grain brown rice with the addition of koji (fermented rice), this is a naturally sweet nectar-like drink containing no alcohol, sugar, or salt. Amazake can be a snack, a dessert drink, or blended with fruit or nuts to make a smoothie; some beverage and dressing recipes in this book use this delicious, nutritional product.

Egg Substitute

There are different brands of egg substitute on the market; they are made with water, dried plums, and lecithin. Use this substitute in cooking, baking, and preparing salad dressings.

Fruit

Whenever I advise patients to limit or omit certain fruits or fruit juices from their diets, they are surprised. Many diets or cookbooks advocate almost unlimited use of fruit, but there are potential health problems related to overuse of fruit or fruit juice.

One problem with fruit is that it increases coldness in the body, which can unbalance your whole system and prolong the healing process if you are ill or recovering from sickness. Be especially careful about fruit consumption when the climate is damp and humid; dampness and humidity are stressful on the spleen, which makes digesting fruit even more difficult. High-acid fruits are the worst culprits in this regard.

Overconsumption of fruit strains the body's metabolism and can be related to fatigue, excessive mucus, frequent and sticky bowel movements, indigestion, cold hands and feet, painful menstruation or PMS, joint and back pains, and stiff neck.

Another health concern is that most growers wax their fruit to make it appealing to the eye, thereby sealing in any pesticides or fertilizers remaining on the fruit. In order not to ingest these chemicals, look for organic, unwaxed fruit.

Miso

Miso is an unpasteurized fermented food in the form of a paste containing lactobacillus, which is vital to digestion. Miso is often the stock base in vegetarian soups and is also used for spreads, dips, and sauces. It can be made from chick peas, brown rice, soybeans, and other protein foods. Salt is usually added.

Mochi

Mochi is a traditional Japanese food made from a special short-grain sweet rice. Baked, it puffs up into a sort of moist, chewy muffin with a crisp crust. This food is high in carbohydrates and makes a healthy snack.

Nutritional Yeast

The most popular nutritional yeast is *Sacchoaromyces cerevisias*, which is grown on a molasses base. It contains B vitamins and valuable protein containing all the essential amino acids. This yeast's golden-yellow color is from the riboflavin content.

This is a versatile ingredient found in numerous vegetarian dishes. It's easily digested and of great benefit to the body's middle burner (stomach and spleen). Old and young alike can enjoy it in the form of flakes or powder; flakes are equivalent to one-half the amount of powder. Use this great energy booster in salads, soups, dressings, popcorn, or other dishes that can use its nutty flavor. It has a long shelf life if kept in a cool dark place.

Oil

Oil is called for in a number of recipes in this book; use high-quality, cold pressed vegetable oil with no cholesterol content. Canola, safflower, olive, and sesame oil are all possibilities.

Preserved Cabbage

Use preserved cabbage instead of onions, garlic, chives, scallions, or shallots. You can purchase it at an oriental grocery; read the label to make sure the cabbage is packed only with salt (some brands also contain onion and garlic).

To remove any dirt left in the cabbage, first soak it in a bowl of water. After thoroughly rinsing, squeeze all the water out and spread the cabbage on a clean cloth and let it sit in the sun for two hours to dry. You can also dry it on a tray for two hours in an oven set to low heat. The resulting product is similar to fried onions in texture and taste.

Salt

Some salt intake is important for a healthy body, but it is important to consume the right kind of salt. Most salt used in households and restaurants is refined salt from which naturally occurring healthful minerals have been bleached away. Even some sea salts are subject to processing and refining that remove essential nutrients. Look in your health food store for a real salt which still retains all its natural minerals—Celtic sea salt is one such variety. When I recommend "real salt" in recipes, I am referring to sea salt from which the nutrients have not been bleached or processed away.

Seaweed

Seaweeds are tops when it comes to providing magnesium, iron, iodine, and sodium. They also have healthy amounts of calcium and phosphorous. Seaweeds are low-calorie protein foods with a very low fat content, and they provide all the trace minerals required by the body. Seaweeds' high mineral and alkaline contents purify the blood by eliminating acidic effects of other foods and dissolving fat deposits. And seaweeds are high in vitamin B12, which assists in proper functioning of the neuro-muscular system; a deficiency of this vitamin can result in pernicious anemia.

Seaweed products are available in a wide variety. Milder flavor seaweeds include dulse, kombu, arame, and nori. Kelp, wakame, and hijiki all have a stronger taste. Seaweed is sold in its dried form; soak it before you use it and save the water to use in cooking grains or soups.

Seitan

Seitan is a protein product made from wheat. Starch is removed from the wheat flour by combining it with water and kneading the resulting dough several times. Once cooked, seitan has a chewy texture similar to meat. As a protein food, it's used in many vegetarian recipes and is readily available at health food stores.

Soy Sauce (Shoyu)

Soy sauce is a delicious substitute for salt, made from wheat, soybeans, water, and real salt. Tamari is a wheat-free version of soy sauce; Bragg Amino Sauce® is soy-free. You can buy low-sodium soy sauce or dilute it with water or simply use it sparingly to reduce the saltiness.

Sweeteners

Occasional use of sweeteners is part of vegetarian cooking. Raw sugar, molasses, or granulated can juice (Sucanat®) are preferred over white sugar or honey. Stevia, a naturally occurring plant in Latin America and the American Southwest, is an alternative sweetener that has been used in South American countries for centuries and is now widely used in Japan. It is much sweeter than sugar and has no calories.

Research on stevia indicates that it helps regulate blood sugar and can be safely used by hypoglycemic patients. Stevia increases energy levels and mental acuity; it helps regulate blood pressure and can assist in weight loss. It also aids digestion and can soothe upset stomachs. Stevia actually inhibits the growth of bacteria that cause tooth decay instead of promoting bacterial growth as sugar does.

Tempeh

Tempeh is a soy product and has been a staple food for centuries in Indonesia. It's a fermented food produced by culturing soybeans with a mold called *Rhizopus*. The resulting protein food is rich in riboflavin, niacin, and vitamin B6. The fermentation process makes tempeh's protein easily digestible, so it can be useful in the diets of weak or elderly people.

Tofu

Most vegetarian diets call for tofu as a staple food. Made from soybeans, it has been a primary food for millions of people throughout Asia for centuries. Tofu contains high-quality protein, no cholesterol, is low in calories, and is a very inexpensive source of protein. It can be kept fresh in the refrigerator for a week providing it's stored in water that is changed daily. When the tofu begins to have a slightly sour smell, it is starting to go bad. Purchasing tofu in a vacuum-sealed package extends its life; packaging will usually indicate an expiration date.

The recipe section contains a number of tofu recipes; listed below are some very common ways of using tofu.

- Fresh tofu can be eaten raw or added to almost any cooked dish.

- Freezing tofu will add air pockets and toughen it; the texture becomes sponge-like and chewy. Once thawed, it can be added to soups, baked dishes, stir-fried with vegetables, or used as a base ingredient for vegetarian burgers.

- You can also bake fresh firm tofu. Place ½-inch thick slabs on a sheet and bake them at 350 degrees for 20 minutes or until golden-yellow in color. Eat as is or add to any recipe. For regular use, baking is a better preparation method than deep-frying.

- Finally, it's nice to add some variety by occasionally deep-frying tofu for use alone or in recipes. Deep-fried and baked tofu are sometimes sold in health food stores and oriental groceries.

TVP (Textured Vegetable Protein)

TVP is made from soy flour cooked under pressure to extract the oil. It is a protein food free of fat and cholesterol, low in sodium, high in potassium, and fortified with vitamin B12 .

TVP is available as small granules or large chunks. The dried product is rehydrated and can be cooked in any recipes calling for ground meat; the chunks are good in stews, fajitas, kebobs, and pot pies. TVP adds character without adding many calories to a wide variety of vegetarian dishes.

Vegenaises

A taste and texture similar to mayonnaise is found in this eggless, dairy-free product. It contains no sugar, is low in sodium and saturated fat, and has no cholesterol. Use it in dips or as a healthful sandwich spread.

Vegetable Broth

There are a number of ready-made vegetable broth products on the market which are useful for soups and stir-fry. Instant vegetable gravy is also available. These foods are made from soybeans, alfalfa, and whole wheat.

You will find that virtually every product in meat-eating diets has a healthful substitute in vegetarian cooking. Vegetarian food doesn't have to be bland or boring; by using the amazing variety of foods available you can enjoy a wealth of new tastes and textures and find endless opportunities to cook both simply and creatively.

Femininity and the Art of Cooking

As the oldest daughter in my family, I had many responsibilities for taking care of my eleven brothers and sisters, including cooking. I learned to cook at age twelve. In Vietnam, I carried water from the river for our cooking and washing. We had no refrigeration, and I went to the market every morning—fresh foods on a daily basis were almost a must for Vietnamese families.

Our stove consisted of three bricks arranged in a triangle over a small hole, with fire fueled by the dry branches we collected. I remember cooking while my eyes burned from the smoke of the fire and tears ran down my cheeks. I never knew where the soot marks would appear on my face as I wiped away the tears, and I was often soaked with sweat from standing over the hot fire in Vietnam's humid climate, where the temperature can reach 110 degrees.

As I grew up, my grandmother instilled in me many qualities of being female, and many of her tales brightened my soul as I fanned the open fire in our backyard. I will never forget one of the stories she told me concerning the importance of cooking.

Once there was a man who worked in the big city and only came home to his house in the country on weekends. While he was away from home, he fell in love with his secretary, who always came to work wearing make-up, expensive clothing, and perfume. He thought of trading his old plain wife at home for this beautiful city woman.

71

One weekend he came home and decided to break the sad news to his wife. The next morning, as usual, his wife got up early to prepare a special brunch to welcome her husband home and to nurture his health since he had to work so hard to support his family. The smell of the food cooking in the kitchen wafted to the bedroom and awoke the husband. He arose to investigate the wonderful aroma.

In the kitchen, he stood behind his wife and watched. The cooking fire warmed his heart as he watched his wife's old worn hands skillfully stir the delicious vegetables in the frying pan. The color of the foods, the aromas, and the warmth of the fire mingled with his mixed thoughts. With some reluctance, he reached out and put his hand on his wife's shoulder.

His wife was startled. She turned around and her eyes brightened as she gave her husband a loving look. She put her arms around him. At that very moment, the husband realized that he had forgotten how beautiful his wife was. The cooking fire colored her cheeks pink, and her black eyes sparkled as the sun peeked through the thatched roof. He embraced her fragile body as he first had twenty years ago.

My grandmother closed this story with the statement, "This proves the point that the way to a man's heart is through his stomach." But in America, the countless restaurants and food establishments attest to the preference of our society—we would rather eat out.

Our upbringing and education stress earning a big paycheck instead of focusing on real quality of life. The car we drive or the clothes we wear seem to be more important than a solid foundation for ourselves or our families. Cooking is an essential ingredient of the groundwork on which our whole lives rest.

I've sadly discovered that the majority of American women I encounter don't know how to cook and prefer not to spend time in the kitchen. This is ironic since what we eat determines our own level of energy and well-being as well as that of each member of our family. Good cooking and diet are essential to successful living in any domain. In fact, health is wealth.

Some of us fear cooking because of a lack of guidance and knowledge. In this respect, I've tried to provide some direction based on my own experience and that of my clients in regard to healthy cooking and eating. Cooking is rewarding and fun in many ways, and it is a useful tool for self-reflection and quietude. We often wish we could slow down and relax our pace for a few minutes; cooking simple, pleasing meals can provide a welcome break in a hectic schedule.

Cooking helps us develop patience and stimulates our creativity. There is a magic in cooking that can bring out our artistic qualities as we transform vegetables into soups or salads, blocks of tofu into stir-fry or casseroles, and legumes into colorful chili or ragout.

The aromas of herbs and seasonings can ease our tensions. Golden moist muffins and loaves of homemade bread transform our awareness. Nutty steamed brown rice gives a feeling of comfort. In the role of cook, a woman can feel pride and fulfillment in nurturing herself and her family, and so can a man. Cooking brings forth, refines, and rewards the feminine qualities within.

RECIPES
FOR
HIGH-ENERGY
LIVING

Using the Recipes

To be successful at anything, we need to provide our bodies the energy they need all day long. Give your body serious credit for all it does by paying careful attention to what you feed it. This can only improve all the projects and activities you undertake—deadlines can become opportunities to be successfully creative instead of being monsters of stress and debilitation. The recipes in this book can start you on a new path or enrich the vegetarian diet you're already following for healthy, energized living.

A few tips before we start the recipes:

- Never skip breakfast; it refortifies body and soul each morning. Lots of interesting options for this meal are provided.

- Lunch can include any of the main-dish recipes or a hearty sandwich along with your choice of soup or salad.

- Dinner can be the same food as lunch if time is short, or it can be a multicourse meal. Try to cook just enough for one day; it's better to be a little short of food than to have too many leftovers. There are plenty of quick, uncomplicated main dishes if your time is limited.

- Dessert isn't necessary, but feel free to indulge with something sweet on occasion.

- Always try to use organic foods, whether fresh, frozen, canned, or packaged. If it is impossible to find organic ingredients, look for foods with the fewest additives possible.

- If you eat leftovers, include fresh cooked rice or freshly prepared soup or salad to ensure a healthy meal.

- It's advisable to eat a larger lunch and lighter dinner, especially if you wish to stay trim or lose a few pounds.

The recipes in this book are simple and quick to prepare; they are of my own creation as well as modifications of recipes from other sources. Both time-pressed people and those who have more leisure to cook will enjoy them. Please bring them into your kitchen as you expand your vegetarian awareness and repertoire. And remember that the state of your mind is as important to your cooking and your health as any recipe. Take a few minutes to breathe deeply and relax before you cook or eat so your food will be well absorbed to fuel the energy of body, mind, and spirit.

KEEPING YOUR ENERGY UP

Too many of us seem to neglect the most important meal of the day—breakfast. Sleep is a time of bodily purification and rejuvenation as well as a period of fasting. During sleep, as a result of the five levels of purification, toxins accumulate in the stomach (this is discussed in my book *The Simple Path to Health*, Rudra Press, 1995). Drinking a glass of warm water first thing in the morning serves to push the remainder of the toxins out of your system and gives your body a fresh start; a small amount of lemon or lime juice can be added to the warm water if you like.

We need to eat a nourishing breakfast to replenish the body and give us energy to start the day. Foods rich in carbohydrates are highly recommended for breakfast; whole grain breads and pancake mixes are tasty. Nut butters as well as natural fruit spreads, cottage tofu, or vegenaise are great toppings. Of course, maple syrup is good on whole grain pancakes. People suffering from lower back pain and low levels of energy will benefit from a bowl of warm cereal. You can add variety with rice milk, pine nuts, and raisins. Stevia adds sweetness. Fresh fruit and hot tea bring hearty satisfaction and help keep your energy level up.

Fresh cooked rice eaten daily enhances blood and energy flow and eliminates bodily stagnation. Rice opens the body's energetic channels due to its warm nature. It's a great food to include with lunch or dinner and is fine for breakfast too!

There are many varieties of rice, each with its own special taste and consistency. These include short- and long-grain brown rice, sweet rice, wild rice, basmati rice, white rice, red rice, and more. For people with weak digestive tracts, sweet or basmati rice is the best choice. However, many people find brown rice the most filling and satisfying. A combination of equal parts short-grain brown rice and sweet rice makes a tasty dish.

Brown rice takes longer to cook than other kinds and requires more water. Soaking the rice for a few hours reduces cooking time and makes the cooked rice softer. If you use a rice cooker, make sure the inner pan is not aluminum; long-term use of aluminum may be hazardous to your health.

Sample Menus

To help you think about putting together delicious and whole-some vegetarian meals, I've included five days of sample menus for people with limited time and a different five-day menu plan for those who may have more time to spend in the kitchen. The menus include many recipes from this book as well as items you can easily buy at your health food store or grocer's.

It's best to plan your weekly menu in advance and put it on the refrigerator door to organize your shopping and provide an overview for making sure you're eating a well-rounded diet. Your menu is also a reminder to maintain your commitment to vege-tarian meals, especially at the end of the day when you might be tired and tempted to return to less healthy habits.

Most of the recipes in this book take from about 10 to 25 min-utes to prepare. In many cases, an entire meal including soup, rice, and a stir-fry dish takes about 45 minutes preparation time. The same meal can be made in about 25 minutes if white rice is used instead of brown rice.

The following pages of sample menus are meant to spark your own creativity in putting recipes together in a healthy and inven-tive way. Feel free to use the menus as a jumping-off point for your exploration and enjoyment of all the rest of the recipes in this book. Bon appetit!

Five-Day Menu Plan
for People with Limited Time

FIRST DAY

Breakfast

Bowl of warm oat bran cereal

Whole grain bread or toast
with almond butter

Soy milk or hot tea

Lunch

Tempeh sandwich with fresh
tomato, sprouts, and romaine
lettuce

Fresh pear

Mineral water

Dinner

Corn and spinach soup

Soybean patties

Brown rice

Vanilla milkshake for dessert

SECOND DAY

Breakfast

Cream of buckwheat cereal

Pumpkin muffin

Banana

Hot tea

Lunch

Avocado special sandwich

Cabbage salad

Fresh plums

Hot tea

Dinner

Vegetarian pizza

Bean sprout salad

Pineapple sherbet

Hot herbal tea

THIRD DAY

Breakfast

Tofu on the run

Fresh fruit

Hot tea

Lunch

Avocado special sandwich

Blueberry oatmeal muffin

Hot tea or soy milk

Dinner

"Chicken" korma

Brown rice with cumin

Lentil soup

Fresh salad

FOURTH DAY

Breakfast
Lentil soup
　(left over from night's dinner)
Whole grain toast
Banana smoothie

Lunch
Macadamia nut supreme
　sandwich
Tomato orange salad
Mineral water

Dinner
High-energy sesame mix
Steamed broccoli and carrots
Brown rice
Nectarine
Hot herbal tea

FIFTH DAY

Breakfast
Tofu or soy links
Almond rice bread toast
Pear
Hot ginger tea

Lunch
Sandwich express
Fresh fruit
Soy milk or rice milk

Dinner
Sweet peas with tofu
Zucchini and eggplant combo
Brown rice
Fresh pineapple
Hot herbal tea

FIVE-DAY MENU PLAN
FOR PEOPLE WITH MORE TIME
FOR COOKING

FIRST DAY

Breakfast
Bowl of teff or 9-grain cereal
Whole grain bread with tahini
Banana
Soy milk or hot tea

Lunch
Watercress soup
Vegetarian lasagna
Banana smoothie

Dinner
Watercress soup
   (use it up from lunch)
Asparagus and tofu stir-fry
Fresh orange
Hot herbal tea

SECOND DAY

Breakfast
Whole wheat pancakes with
   maple syrup
Strawberries
Hot tea

Lunch
Tomato orange salad
Fried rice
Orange
Hot tea

Dinner
Country kettle soup
Brown rice with cumin
Tofu cheesecake
Hot herbal tea

THIRD DAY

Breakfast
Cottage tofu sandwich
Fresh fruit
Hot tea

Lunch
Brown rice with yams
   (make extra for dinner)
Okra masala
Spinach salad
Homemade soy milk

Dinner

Brown rice with yams
  (left over from lunch)

Oriental miso soup

Fresh orange

Hot herbal tea

FOURTH DAY

Breakfast

Whole grain toast with
  almond butter

Carob brownies

Banana sesame amazake drink

Lunch

Stir-fry rice noodles

Fresh or dried papaya

Hot tea

Dinner

Sweet potato soup

Tofu salad

Fat free figs and nut bread

Pineapple sherbet

Hot herbal tea

FIFTH DAY

Breakfast

Warm cream of rye
  with almonds and raisins

Avocado smoothie

Hot tea

Lunch

Stuffed lemongrass tofu

Brown rice with aduki beans
  (make enough for dinner)

Sweet and sour pineapple
  (make enough for dinner)

Hot tea

Dinner

Barbecued seitan

Brown rice with aduki beans
  (left over from lunch)

Seaweed with green vegetables

Sweet and sour pineapple
  (left over from lunch)

Hot herbal tea

Breads, Cereals, and Pancakes

BANANA NUT MUFFINS

1½ cups whole grain flour

½ teaspoon real salt

1 teaspoon non-aluminum baking powder

1 teaspoon baking soda

½ cup chopped nuts

3 large ripe bananas

½ cup raw sugar

1 cup soy milk

⅓ cup safflower oil

Preheat oven to 375 degrees.

Sift together the dry ingredients and stir in chopped nuts.

Blend the bananas, sugar, soy milk, and oil together in a blender until smooth.

In a mixing bowl, combine the dry and wet ingredients and mix until moist. Fill oiled muffin tins ¾ full; bake for 20 minutes.

Makes 8 muffins

BLUE CORN MUFFINS

1 cup soy milk

1 teaspoon lemon juice

¼ cup vegetable oil

⅓ cup honey

1 cup blue cornmeal

1 cup whole wheat pastry flour

½ teaspoon baking soda

1 teaspoon non-aluminum baking powder

Preheat over to 375 degrees.

In a small bowl, blend soy milk, lemon juice, oil, and honey.

In a larger bowl, combine remaining ingredients. Stir liquid into dry ingredients until moist. Fill oiled muffin tins ¾ full and bake for about 18 minutes.

Makes 8 muffins

BLUEBERRY OATMEAL MUFFINS

1 cup teff or other whole grain flour

2 teaspoons non-aluminum baking powder

½ teaspoon real salt

½ teaspoon cinnamon

½ cup raw sugar

1 cup rolled oats

1½ cups soy milk

¼ cup melted canola oil margarine

¾ cup blueberries

Preheat oven to 375 degrees.

Stir dry ingredients together, adding sugar and rolled oats last.

In another bowl, mix together soy milk and margarine, then add dry ingredients and stir until moist. Fold in the blueberries. Fill oiled muffin tins about ¾ full, and bake for about 20 minutes or until golden brown.

Makes 8 muffins

CARROT BRAN MUFFINS

½ cup teff or whole grain flour

½ cup carrot, finely grated

1 cup oat bran

1 cup safflower oil

¾ cup raw sugar

½ cup raisins or currants

½ cup soy milk

¼ cup molasses

1 teaspoon non-aluminum baking powder

1 teaspoon baking soda

1 teaspoon cinnamon

¼ teaspoon real salt (optional)

Preheat oven to 375 degrees.

In a large bowl, combine all ingredients and mix well. Fill oiled muffin tins about ¾ full, and bake about 25 minutes.

Makes 8 muffins

POPPY SEED MUFFINS

2 cups teff or whole grain flour

2½ teaspoons baking soda

½ teaspoon real salt

¼ teaspoon ground nutmeg

¼ cup softened canola oil margarine

¾ cup raw sugar

½ teaspoon grated orange peel

1½ cups soy milk

½ cup golden raisins

½ cup chopped pecans

5 tablespoons poppy seeds

Preheat oven to 400 degrees.

In a mixing bowl, combine margarine, sugar, and orange peel and blend until smooth.

In a separate bowl, mix together the flour, baking soda, salt, and nutmeg. Slowly add the dry ingredients to the margarine mixture, using the soy milk to blend it all. Fold in raisins, nuts, and seeds.

Spoon batter into oiled muffin tins until cups are ¾ full. Bake for 20 minutes or until golden brown.

Makes 8 muffins

PUMPKIN MUFFINS

SIFT AND MIX TOGETHER:

1½ cups teff or whole grain flour

1½ teaspoons cinnamon

1 teaspoon non-aluminum baking powder

1 teaspoon baking powder

1 teaspoon salt

BLEND UNTIL SMOOTH:

1 cup soy milk

¾ cup raw sugar

½ cup oil

1 cup pumpkin

Preheat oven to 375 degrees.

Combine both mixtures and mix well until smooth. Add 1 cup raisins, if desired. Fill oiled muffin tins about ¾ full and bake for 15–20 minutes.

Makes 8 muffins

FAT-FREE FIGS AND NUT BREAD

½ cup black mission figs, thickly sliced

SIFT TOGETHER AND MIX WELL:

2 cups whole grain flour

½ teaspoon baking soda

2 tablespoons non-aluminum baking powder

1 teaspoon cinnamon

⅛ teaspoon ground cloves

¼ teaspoon nutmeg

BLEND TOGETHER WELL:

¼ cup egg substitute

½ cup maple syrup

2 tablespoons Sucanat sweetener or raw sugar

Preheat oven to 350 degrees.

Sift the dry ingredients together in a bowl and blend the wet ingredients in a blender.

Then slowly add the dry ingredients and the figs to the blender and blend at medium speed until smooth. Bake in oiled bread pan for 45 minutes or until toothpick comes out clean.

8 servings

NUTRITIOUS ZUCCHINI BREAD

2 cups raw zucchini, grated

1 cup pine nuts

SIFT TOGETHER AND MIX THOROUGHLY:

2 cups whole wheat flour

2 teaspoons baking soda *[skp 1tbp B powder]*

1 teaspoon cinnamon

¼ teaspoon cloves

BLEND TOGETHER WELL:

1 cup egg substitute   *1 flax egg 1TBSP + 3TBSP H2O*

⅔ cup mild-flavor molasses *1tsp Sugar*

2 teaspoons vanilla

pinch of real salt *stick one ½ one*

Preheat oven to 350 degrees. *150° – 130°*

In a large bowl, mix together the sifted ingredients and the blended ingredients. Then fold the zucchini and pine nuts into the mixture.

Pour into oiled bread pan and bake for 1 hour or until toothpick comes out clean.   *40–45 mins*

8 servings

EDIE'S HOMEMADE GRANOLA

DRY INGREDIENTS:

1 cup sunflower seeds

1 cup wheat germ

7 cups rolled oats

4 cups puffed rice

1 cup date pieces raisins

1 cup almond pieces

1 cup shredded coconut 1/3 cup

1 cup sesame seeds

WET INGREDIENTS:

1 cup packed raw brown sugar

1 cup safflower oil

½ cup honey

17 ounces natural applesauce

1 tablespoon crushed orange peel

1 tablespoon real vanilla extract

1 teaspoon cinnamon

Preheat oven to 350 degrees.

Mix dry ingredients in a large bowl. Combine room-temperature wet ingredients in a separate bowl, stirring until evenly mixed.

Pour wet ingredients on top of dry ingredients and mix together well.

Spread mixture on a cookie sheet, forming a layer about 1½ inches thick. Bake for 10 minutes, checking frequently. When the top is brown, turn ingredients over with a spatula. Do the same about 3 more times until everything is evenly browned.

Makes about 5 pounds of granola—great for breakfast, snacks, and traveling.

WHOLESOME PROTEIN CEREAL

For a large batch of ready-to-cook dry cereal, use one of the following mixtures. Mix the dry ingredients together and store in an airtight container.

FARMOLA CEREAL

2 cups cracked wheat or cream of wheat

1 cup cornmeal

1 cup cracked rye

1 cup soy flour

MELLOWMEAL CEREAL

4 cups cornmeal

2½ cups soy flour

2½ cups cracked rye

1 cup cracked buckwheat or buckwheat meal

½ cup millet

TO COOK EITHER CEREAL:

Whisk 1 part cereal into 3 parts boiling water. Stir constantly at medium heat for a few minutes while cereal thickens. Reduce heat and continue cooking for 25 minutes, stirring often.

For variety, serve with raisins, fresh fruit, or other condiments.

WHOLE WHEAT PANCAKES

10 ounces soy milk

1 cup whole wheat or teff flour

1 tablespoon soy flour

½ teaspoon baking powder

½ teaspoon cinnamon

1 tablespoon poppy seeds

1 tablespoon unsalted soy margarine

2 tablespoons honey

1 tablespoon grated orange rind

½ cup chopped walnuts

1 tablespoon safflower oil

Combine all dry ingredients in a mixing bowl.

In another large bowl, combine all wet ingredients except the oil. Then mix in the dry ingredients to make a batter.

Heat the oil in a skillet and drop batter by ¼-cup measures to form pancakes. Cook until top is dry; turn and cook the other side briefly. Top with maple syrup or applesauce.

4 servings

Sandwiches

AVOCADO SPECIAL SANDWICH

9-grain or other whole grain bread

1 small avocado, peeled, pitted, and sliced

½ cup carrot, finely grated

⅓ teaspoon real salt

black pepper

vegenaise

Spread bread with vegenaise and assemble ingredients into sandwich.

Makes enough for 2 sandwiches

COTTAGE TOFU SANDWICH

Whole grain bread, spread with almond butter

½ cup cottage tofu (see "Tofu, Tempeh, and Seitan" recipes)

1 cup chopped dandelion greens or other fresh greens

1 small tomato, cubed

1 teaspoon vegenaise

dash of lemon or lime juice

Mix ingredients in a small bowl and spread on almond-buttered bread.

Makes enough for 2 sandwiches

MACADAMIA NUT SUPREME SANDWICH

whole grain bread

macadamia nut butter spread

4 thin tomato slices

½ medium carrot, finely grated

a few fresh mint leaves, finely chopped

alfalfa or sunflower sprouts

mustard

Mix grated carrots and mint leaves with mustard. Spread macadamia nut butter thickly on bread and place tomato slices and carrot mixture on top. Sprinkle generously with sprouts.

Makes enough for 2 sandwiches

SUN SANDWICH

8 slices whole grain bread

4 tablespoons mashed soft tofu

4 teaspoon vegenaise

2 cups roasted sunflower seeds

4 teaspoons carrot, finely grated

2 teaspoons mustard

2 teaspoons nutritional yeast

2 teaspoons fresh chopped parsley

vegetable of choice, such as thinly sliced tomato or zucchini

Mix all ingredients together, spread on toast, and top with vegetables.

Makes 4 sandwiches

SANDWICH EXPRESS

8 slices whole grain bread

4 veggie burgers

4 leaves romaine lettuce

8 thin tomato slices

4 teaspoons canola margarine

4 teaspoons alfalfa or sunflower sprouts

pinch of coriander (optional)

Cook the veggie burgers in a pan or oven according to package instructions. Spread margarine on the bread slices and assemble the sandwiches.

Makes 4 sandwiches

TEMPEH CUTLET SANDWICH

4 whole grain buns

4 precooked tempeh cutlets

8 tomato slices

1 cucumber, peeled and sliced lengthwise

1 cup alfalfa sprouts

1 teaspoon vegenaise or tofu sour cream
    (see recipe in "Salads, Dressings, and Sauces")

Spread vegenaise or tofu sour cream on buns and assemble sandwiches.

Makes 4 sandwiches

TOFU ON THE RUN

whole grain sunflower seed buns, halved and toasted

8 ounces firm tofu, mashed coarsely

½ teaspoon real salt

½ teaspoon pepper

2 tablespoons vegenaise

juice of half a lemon or lime

a few chopped mint leaves or other fresh chopped herb

a few slivered almonds or nuts of your choice as garnish

dash of paprika

Mix all ingredients except nuts and paprika and spread on toasted buns. Sprinkle paprika and nuts on top. This is a quick, easy, and nutritious dish to take on the road.

Makes 4 sandwiches

Soups

AVOCADO CUCUMBER SOUP

1 cup soy milk

1 large avocado, peeled and pitted

1 small cucumber, peeled, seeded, and finely chopped

⅔ cup water

juice from ½ lime

¼ cup cilantro

¼ teaspoon real salt

Place all ingredients except cilantro in blender and blend until smooth. Garnish with chopped cilantro.

This soup has a cold nature; therefore it is best to eat it in summer.

4 servings

ADUKI BEAN SOUP

1 cup aduki beans

1 teaspoon tapioca beads

2 ripe pears, peeled and quartered

6 cups water

tamari sauce to taste

Soak beans overnight (or all day) in cool water and then discard water.

Soak tapioca beads in bowl for 15 minutes in just-boiled water, or cook the tapioca in a covered pan on low heat for 15 minutes. Drain and set aside.

Cook the aduki beans in 6 cups water at medium heat for 1½ hours or until soft; check the beans occasionally and add more water if necessary.

Add pears to the bean pot and bring to a boil. Add tapioca and cook for 3 minutes. Season with tamari.

This soup is excellent for kidney tonification and rejuvenation.

4 servings

BARLEY MUSHROOM SOUP

1 cup barley

2 quarts water

1 small carrot, cubed

1 medium potato, cubed

½ pound fresh shiitake mushrooms, sliced

1 thumb-size piece of ginger, thinly sliced

1 tablespoon canola oil

1 teaspoon sesame oil

2 tablespoons tamari or soy sauce

3 tablespoons fresh coriander, chopped coarsely

Soak the barley for at least 1 hour, then rinse and bring it to a boil in a soup pot with 2 quarts of fresh water. Boil for 20 minutes, add carrot and potato cubes, and simmer for 15 minutes or until potatoes and barley are tender.

Just before serving, sauté ginger and mushrooms in the canola oil and add to the soup.

Mix the sesame oil with the tamari sauce, serve soup into bowls, and drizzle oil mixture on top of the soup. Garnish with coriander.

4 servings

BUTTERNUT SQUASH SOUP

1 medium butternut squash, peeled and cut in 1-inch cubes

1 small sweet potato, peeled and cut in 1-inch cubes

2 teaspoons chick pea miso

5 cups water

roasted sesame seeds for garnish

Place water, potato, and squash pieces in a soup pot and boil for 10 minutes or until pieces are soft. Then put the cooked squash and potato along with their liquid in a blender with the miso and blend until smooth.

Pour into bowls and top with roasted sesame seeds. Serve with rice crackers or whole grain toasted bread.

This soup can be served chilled in summer or warm in winter. It is nutritious and digestible for sick people.

4 servings

CHILI BEAN SOUP

15-ounce can kidney beans

15-ounce can great northern beans

15-ounce can navy beans

15-ounce can pinto beans

4 cups diced tomatoes or 15-ounce can organic crushed tomatoes

4-ounce can tomato paste

1 cup TVP granules (texturized vegetable protein)

½ tablespoon Sucanat sweetener or raw sugar

½ teaspoon cumin

¼ teaspoon sweet basil

1 teaspoon chili powder (or less, depending on taste)

2 quarts water

Place all ingredients in large soup pot and bring to a boil. Reduce heat and simmer at least 30 minutes. Serve with fresh-cooked rice.

This dish is good the second day for freezing if you make extra.

6 servings

CONGEE

1 cup pearl barley, soaked 1 to 2 hours, or 16-ounce can barley

1 cup potatoes, cut in ¼-inch cubes

1 cup carrots, cut in ¼-inch cubes

¼ cup pickled cabbage
   (see recipe in "Vegetable Entrées, and Side Dishes")

6 shiitake mushrooms, soaked and thinly sliced

6 cups water

1 tablespoon nutritional yeast

2 teaspoons vegetable broth powder

dash black pepper

3 teaspoons soy sauce mixed with 3 teaspoons sesame oil

ginger strips for garnish

fresh chopped coriander for garnish

In a soup pot, boil the barley in the water at medium heat for 20 minutes. If you use canned barley, just bring it to a boil, then add other ingredients, including water.

While the barley cooks, mix together the potatoes, carrots, cabbage, and mushrooms in a large bowl. Add this mixture to the cooked barley and continue cooking until potatoes are tender. Add seasonings and cook for 5 more minutes, then stir in soy sauce mixture.

Pour into bowls and garnish with ginger and coriander.

This soup is very beneficial for people suffering from colds, flu, coughs, or asthma. For these conditions, eat a small portion every 2 hours.

6 servings

CORN AND SPINACH SOUP

2 ears corn, kernels cut from cob

3 cups fresh spinach, cut in 1-inch pieces

4 cups water

1 teaspoon tamari

1 teaspoon nutritional yeast

1 teaspoon fresh coriander, finely chopped

Bring water to a boil, add corn and spinach, and turn off heat. Add tamari and yeast; cover and let sit for 5 minutes. Garnish with coriander and serve with cooked rice.

4 servings

COUNTRY KETTLE SOUP

1 cup cooked wild rice

2 medium potatoes, quartered

½ cup TVP granules (texturized vegetable protein)

½ quart soy milk

1 cup soft tofu, crumbled

1 cup carrot curls for garnish

real salt and pepper to taste

Soak the TVP in 1 cup of hot water for 5 minutes to soften it, then drain.

In a saucepan, cover potatoes with plenty of water and boil until tender; drain liquid and mash to creamy consistency. Add TVP, soy milk, and tofu and cook at medium heat, stirring until well blended.

Mix in rice and garnish with carrot curls.

4 servings

HEARTY VEGETABLE SOUP

1 pound ripe chopped tomatoes, or 15-ounce can chunky
  tomato sauce

4 cups cabbage, coarsely chopped

1 carrot, quartered and coarsely chopped

1 cup TVP granules (texturized vegetable protein)

1 bay leaf

1 teaspoon dried thyme leaf

¼ teaspoon paprika

1 teaspoon real salt

1 cup fresh coarsely chopped parsley

4 cups water

1 tablespoons raw sugar

dash of tabasco sauce (optional)

1 cup naturally fermented low-sodium sauerkraut (optional)

In a large stockpot, combine all ingredients except parsley, sugar,
and sauerkraut. Bring to a boil, then reduce heat and simmer in
covered pot for 1 hour.

Add parsley, sugar, and sauerkraut and cook uncovered for addi-
tional 30 minutes.

6 servings

LENTIL SOUP

6 cups water

½ cup lentils

1 medium potato, diced

1 medium carrot, sliced diagonally

1 celery stalk, sliced diagonally

2 ripe tomatoes, diced

1 teaspoon basil

½ teaspoon dried parsley

½ teaspoon salt

1 tablespoon oil

In a stockpot, combine all ingredients except oil and bring to a boil. Reduce heat and simmer for 1 hour or until lentils are tender. Add oil and cook for 2 more minutes.

4 servings

LOTUS SEED & TOFU SOUP

2 cups firm tofu, cubed

2 cups lotus seeds

½ cup fresh green peas

6 cups water

In a saucepan, boil lotus seeds in water until soft but not mushy. Add remaining ingredients and cook at medium heat for 5 minutes. Sprinkle with a favorite herb as garnish.

This soup is good for weak or sick people; it strengthens the heart.

4 servings

MUSHROOM SOUP

5½ cups water

1 pound fresh mushrooms, sliced

1½ teaspoons dried dill

1 teaspoon paprika

1 teaspoon caraway seed (optional)

⅛ teaspoon black pepper

1 teaspoon vegetable broth powder

½ teaspoon real salt

1 cup soy milk

2 teaspoons lemon juice

1 teaspoon olive oil

3 teaspoons flour

In a soup pot, mix together all ingredients except flour, oil, soy milk, and lemon juice. Bring to a boil, reduce heat, and simmer for 15 minutes.

In a separate stockpot, lightly warm the oil, add flour, and cook for 1 minute while stirring constantly. Keeping the heat low, whisk in soy milk and stir until smooth.

Add the mushroom soup to the thickened sauce and simmer for 15 minutes. Just before serving, whisk in lemon juice. Serve with rice.

6 servings

NOODLE SOUP

½ cup baked tofu, thinly sliced

1 cup macaroni or other noodles of your choice

6 cups vegetable broth for soup base (see recipe later in this
section)

1 cup dried shiitake mushrooms, soaked and thinly sliced

tamari sauce to taste

To bake the tofu, place ½-inch-thick slices on a cookie sheet and
bake at 350 degrees for 20 minutes or until golden yellow in
color.

Drop noodles into a large pot of boiling water and boil for about
8–10 minutes or until just tender; drain in colander.

In a soup pot, combine all ingredients, bring to a boil, and cook
for 5 minutes at medium heat.

For variety, you can add any chopped vegetable to this soup; it's
a good dish for sick or weak people.

4 servings

ORIENTAL MISO SOUP

6 cups water

10 inches of wakame seaweed

5 ounces tofu, cut in small cubes

1 teaspoon miso

soy sauce or tamari sauce to taste

Soak wakame to soften it, then cut into ½-inch pieces. Dissolve miso in small bowl of warm water. In a stockpot, bring water to a boil and add all ingredients. Heat for 3 minutes and serve.

4 servings

PEARL BARLEY SOUP

2 cups cooked pearl barley (½ cup dry barley)

6 cups water

1 carrot, thinly sliced

½ cup spinach

1 teaspoon sesame oil

tamari sauce to taste

Wash and rinse the dry barley. Bring 2 cups water to a boil, add barley, reduce heat, and cook for about 45 minutes.

Put cooked barley, remaining water, and carrots in a stockpot, bring to a boil, reduce heat, and simmer for 15 minutes.

Add spinach, oil, and tamari and bring to a boil again before serving.

This soup nourishes and strengthens the spleen, stomach, lungs, and kidneys. It's good for children and for those recovering from prolonged illness.

4 servings

RED LENTIL SOUP

1 cup red lentils

1 carrot, diced

⅔ teaspoon vegetable broth powder or instant gravy

1 teaspoon cumin

1 teaspoon canola margarine

4 cups water

Rinse the lentils thoroughly to remove any grit or small pebbles. In a soup pot, bring water, lentils, and carrots to a boil. Reduce heat and simmer for 1 hour; add more water for a thinner soup.

Add cumin and instant gravy; bring to a boil again. Before serving, dot with the margarine. Serve with cooked rice.

4 servings

SPLIT PEA SOUP

½ cup dried split peas

2 cups water

1 stalk celery, thinly sliced

1 medium carrot, thinly sliced

1 bay leaf

real salt to taste

Combine all ingredients in a medium pot and boil for 20 minutes. Reduce heat and simmer until split peas are tender. Top with favorite fresh herb.

4 servings

SPINACH SOUP

2 cups fresh spinach, cut in 2-inch pieces

1 tablespoon TVP granules (texturized vegetable protein)

5 fresh mushrooms, thinly sliced

3 cups water

1 teaspoon nutritional yeast

1 teaspoon vegetable broth powder

1 tablespoon fresh coriander, coarsely chopped

Soak the TVP in a little hot water for 5 minutes to soften it, then drain. Add the mushrooms and TVP to boiling water, then mix in all other ingredients and turn off heat. Serve right away.

4 servings

STUFFED BITTER MELON SOUP

2 medium bitter melons, slit ¾ open lengthwise and seeded

1½-ounce package bean thread, cut in 1-inch pieces

5 shiitake mushrooms, soaked in hot water and minced

2 tablespoons TVP granules (texturized vegetable protein)

½ pound tofu, crumbled

2 teaspoons nutritional yeast

10 peppercorns (optional)

1 teaspoon preserved cabbage

1 teaspoon soy sauce

5 drops stevia

6 cups water

fresh chopped coriander for garnish

Cover the bean thread with hot water and soak for 5 minutes, then drain. In a separate bowl, soak the TVP in 4 tablespoons of hot water for 5 minutes and drain.

In a large bowl, mix together all ingredients except bitter melons. In a soup pot, bring the water to a boil.

While water is coming to a boil, stuff the melons with mixture from the bowl, then carefully put the melons into the boiling water. Turn heat to medium low, cover, and simmer for 25 minutes.

Remove melons to a cutting board and cut into inch-long pieces. Place melon pieces in bowls, cover with hot broth, and garnish with coriander. For a meal, serve with rice and a protein dish.

4 servings

SWEET POTATO SOUP

2 cups raw sweet potato, peeled and cubed

½ cup celery, thickly sliced

½ cup carrots, thinly sliced

¼ cup fresh parsley, chopped

¼ cup fresh cilantro, chopped

4 cups vegetable broth for soup base (see recipe later in this section)

2 tablespoons virgin olive oil

1½ teaspoons ground coriander

½ teaspoon ground thyme

1 cup soy milk

real salt and pepper to taste

In a soup pot, sauté vegetables, parsley, and coriander in olive oil for 5 minutes or until vegetables are soft.

Add broth, coriander, and thyme and bring to a boil. Reduce heat, cover, and simmer for 1 hour.

Add soy milk, salt, and pepper and simmer a few more minutes. For a creamy soup, purée in a blender before adding soy milk, salt, and pepper; then briefly warm again in soup pot.

Serve with fresh whole grain bread.

6 servings

VEGETABLE BROTH FOR SOUP BASE

2 medium carrots, sliced 1 inch thick

1 bunch carrot greens, cut in 1-inch pieces

1 ear of corn, kernels cut from cob

6 cups water

In a soup pot, combine all ingredients and cook for 1 hour at medium heat. Strain and discard all solids. Remaining broth can be used as a base in any soup.

4 servings

VEGETABLE CHOWDER

3 cups potatoes, peeled and diced

1½ cups whole kernel corn

3 cups tomatoes, diced

½ cup celery, sliced thinly

4 cups water

2 cups soy milk

real salt to taste

fresh parsley to garnish

In a large pot, combine all ingredients except soy milk. Bring to a boil, then reduce heat and simmer until vegetables are tender.

Add soy milk and continue simmering until heated through. Serve topped with fresh parsley.

4 servings

VEGETARIAN BROTH

4 carrots, thinly sliced

2 large tomatoes, diced

2 large parsnips, diced

2 large potatoes, diced

4 stalks celery, thinly sliced

2 pears, peeled and quartered

10 cups water

1 bay leaf

1 small bouquet fresh parsley, thyme, and dill tied together

2 to 6 peppercorns

real salt to taste

Place all ingredients in large stockpot and bring to a boil. Reduce heat to medium low and simmer for 1½ hours.

Strain broth and discard all solid remainders. Return broth to a boil and continue cooking until liquid equals about 4 cups.

This is an excellent broth for sick or weak people.

4 servings

WATERCRESS SOUP

1 bunch watercress

½ cup baked tofu, cut in ½-inch slices

3 cups water

1 teaspoon vegetable seasoning or instant gravy

1 teaspoon canola oil

soy sauce or tamari sauce to taste

To bake the tofu, place ½-inch-thick slices on a cookie sheet and bake at 350 degrees for 20 minutes or until golden yellow in color.

Boil water in medium pot, add all ingredients, and cook for 1 minute. Remove pot from heat, let stand for 2 minutes, and serve.

4 servings

ZUCCHINI SOUP

1 medium zucchini, cut in ⅓-inch diagonal slices

4 dried shiitake mushrooms, soaked and sliced, or 6 fresh
  shiitake mushrooms, sliced

3 ounces tofu

4 cups water

1 tablespoon canola oil

In a soup pot, bring water to a boil and add all ingredients. Cook
for 5 minutes and serve with whole grain bread.

4 servings

Herbal Soups

The following soups are meant especially to strengthen blood and energy. If you or somebody you know is sick, weak, or tired, these recipes will help. They are based on traditional Chinese medicine and have been used with success for centuries. The herbs, though unfamiliar to most Westerners, can be found at Chinese herb stores or oriental grocery stores.

BLOOD TONIFYING SOUP

10 2-inch slices dried radix asparagi

10 2-inch slices dried radix glehniae

2 tablespoons radix ophiopogonas

10 dried and pitted red dates

8 cups water

In a large pot, combine all ingredients and cook for 30–60 minutes at medium-low heat.

Consume both broth and herbs for their tonic effect.

4 servings

HEALTHY KIDNEY & LIVER SOUP

10 2-inch slices dried radix glehniae

1 tablespoon radix ophiopogonas

1 tablespoon fructus mori

10 2-inch slices dried radix asparagi

8 cups water

In a large saucepan, combine ingredients and simmer for 30–60 minutes. Drink the remaining juice.

The herbs can be used once more for this soup by adding another 7 cups water and simmering for another hour.

This soup is good for strengthening the kidneys and liver.

4 servings

HWANG QI SOUP

8 ounces seitan

1 quart water

2 medium potatoes, cubed

2 grams astragalus

1 teaspoon ginger juice

real salt or tamari to taste

Combine all ingredients in a pot and cook at medium heat for 45 minutes. Add water as needed to maintain a soup consistency.

Astragalus increases energy levels and strengthens the immune system.

4 servings

TONIC SOUP

2 quarts water

8 2-inch slices astragalus

8 2-inch slices dioscorea

1 cup lotus seeds

4 short pieces codonopsis

5 pieces dried black fungus

5 thin slices ginger

¼ cup polygonum

¼ cup lychium fruit

1 tablespoon longan fruit

1 tablespoon black hair-like seaweed

In a soup pot, combine all ingredients except seaweed and cook for 1 hour at medium heat. Use a ceramic pot, if possible. If water gets too low, add more. Season with a dash of real salt or tamari. Add the seaweed for the last 3 minutes of cooking.

This soup has multiple medicinal effects: astragalus, codonopsis, and dioscorea increase energy and strengthen the immune system. Polygonum, lychium fruit, and longan fruit nurture the body and strengthen the blood. Lotus seed is an astringent which strengthens heart and kidneys. Black fungus cools the blood and boosts energy; seaweed is moistening and strengthens yin; ginger disperses cold.

8 servings

Salads, Dressings, and Sauces

BEAN SPROUT SALAD

1½ cups fresh bean sprouts

1 medium head Boston or butter lettuce, torn into bite-size
pieces

1 medium cucumber, seeded and thinly sliced

10 fresh strawberries, halved

1 teaspoon nutritional yeast

Combine all ingredients, toss, and top with Quick and Easy Salad
Dressing (see recipe in this section).

Serves 4

CABBAGE SALAD

2 pounds cabbage, shredded

1 cup baked tofu, thinly sliced

¼ cup tomato, peeled and diced

1 cup fresh orange juice

2 tablespoons oil

1 tablespoon soy sauce

½ cup roasted peanuts, chopped in small pieces

real salt

pepper

pinch of oregano

pinch of basil

fresh chopped cilantro (optional)

To bake the tofu, place ½-inch-thick slices of firm tofu on a sheet and bake them at 350 degrees for 20 minutes or until golden yellow in color.

In a large bowl, sprinkle salt onto cabbage and pour hot water over top; let stand 10 minutes. Drain cabbage in a colander, press out excess water, and set aside.

In another bowl, combine tomato, orange juice, oil, and soy sauce; add seasonings to taste. Add tofu, then cabbage, and toss. Top with chopped peanuts.

Serves 4

EGGLESS EGG SALAD

15 ounces soft tofu

1½ teaspoons apple cider vinegar

3 teaspoons mustard

1½ teaspoons raw sugar or honey (optional)

¾ teaspoon turmeric

3 tablespoons celery, diced

1½ teaspoons parsley, chopped

dash of paprika

pepper to taste

Crumble tofu in mixing bowl. In a separate bowl, combine vinegar, mustard, sugar, and turmeric. Mix thoroughly and pour over tofu. Add celery, parsley, paprika, and pepper. Mix thoroughly.

Refrigerate 30 minutes to allow flavors to meld. Serve on top of fresh garden greens or use as a sandwich spread.

Serves 4

OLIVE PASTA SALAD

3 cups cooked macaroni or shell pasta

½ cup green pepper, chopped finely

⅓ cup pimento, chopped finely

½ cup fresh parsley, chopped finely

½ cup soy cheese or firm tofu, grated or crumbled

1 cup olives, sliced

¼ cup oil

¼ cup roasted sesame seeds

1 tablespoon lemon juice

¾ teaspoon real salt

¾ teaspoon thyme or lemon thyme

¼ teaspoon sweet basil

Cook enough dry pasta to make 3 cups cooked product. Toss pasta, green pepper, pimento, parsley, soy cheese, and olives together in large bowl.

In a separate bowl, blend oil and seasonings together, and add dressing to salad. Toss all ingredients, chill, and serve.

Serves 6

SPINACH SALAD

1 pound young spinach leaves, cut into 1-inch pieces

1 stalk celery, thinly sliced

½ cup pine nuts

½ cup black olives

5 tablespoons olive oil

2 tablespoons apple cider vinegar or ½ cup fresh orange juice

1 tablespoon tamari

½ teaspoon mustard powder

In a large bowl, combine all ingredients; toss and serve.

Serves 6

TEMPEH SALAD

8 ounces tempeh, finely chopped

½ cup cucumber, finely chopped

½ cup tomato, finely chopped

½ cup carrot, shredded

¼ cup mushroom, finely chopped

2 or 3 tablespoons vegenaise or tofu sour cream

1 tablespoon soy sauce or tamari

1 teaspoon basil

1 teaspoon parsley

½ teaspoon horseradish

½ teaspoon mustard

In a large bowl, mix all ingredients together; serve on lettuce leaves or use as a sandwich spread on whole grain bread.

Serves 6

TOFU SALAD

1 cup baked tofu, thinly sliced

5 tablespoons olive oil

2 tablespoons vinegar

½ teaspoon oregano

½ teaspoon basil

¼ teaspoon ground bay leaf

real salt and pepper

1 cucumber, thinly sliced

2 medium tomatoes, cut in small wedges

4 leaves romaine lettuce, cut in 1-inch pieces

15 black olives

¼ teaspoon stevia (optional)

Preheat oven to 350 degrees. Place ½-inch-thick slices of firm tofu on a baking sheet and bake for 20 minutes or until tofu is golden yellow in color.

In a large bowl, mix together oil, vinegar, oregano, basil, bay leaf, salt, and pepper. Add the cucumber, tomato, lettuce, and olives and toss.

Serves 6

TOMATO ORANGE SALAD

2 medium ripe tomatoes, peeled, seeded, and cubed

10 leaves romaine lettuce, cut into 1-inch pieces

3 naval oranges, peeled, seeded, and thinly sliced

½ cup fresh dill, finely chopped

1 tablespoon tamari sauce

real salt and pepper to taste

Combine ingredients in large bowl, toss, and serve.

Serves 6

AMAZAKE SALAD DRESSING

1 cup plain amazake

½ cup vegenaise

2 tablespoons vinegar

1 tablespoon red miso (any miso is acceptable)

Combine all ingredients in a blender and process until smooth. Then dress up your favorite salad!

CREAMY BASIL DRESSING

4 ounces soy milk

juice of 1 lime

6 leaves of fresh basil

1 tablespoon olive oil

1 tablespoon vegetable oil

½ teaspoon thyme

½ teaspoon dill

dash of black pepper

dash of cayenne pepper

dash of real salt

Combine soy milk, lime juice, and basil in a blender until mixed together, then slowly blend in oils a few drops at a time. Add remaining ingredients and blend for a few more seconds.

MISO SALAD DRESSING

2 tablespoons chick pea miso

1 teaspoon fresh ginger, minced

1 tablespoon raw sugar

2 tablespoons warm water

½ cup oil

2 tablespoons vinegar or fresh lime juice

In a small bowl, thoroughly whisk together all ingredients.

QUICK AND EASY DRESSING

1 cup fresh orange juice

1 tablespoon tamari sauce

1 tablespoon olive oil

1 teaspoon fresh dill

Mix ingredients thoroughly and use on any salad.

SOY MILK SALAD DRESSING

½ cup soy milk

¼ cup oil

½ teaspoon lemon juice

2 tablespoons raw sugar

dash of real salt

Thoroughly combine all ingredients in a blender. Chill and use on any salad or as a coleslaw dressing.

BARBECUE SAUCE

2 cups tomato sauce

¼ cup oil

¼ cup water

2 tablespoons raw sugar

1 tablespoon molasses

½ cup mustard

1 teaspoon allspice

2 teaspoons ground red pepper

2 tablespoons minced parsley

1 tablespoon tamari sauce

¼ cup lemon juice

In a saucepan, combine all ingredients except tamari and lemon juice. Cook at medium-low heat for 45 minutes, stirring occasionally. Stir in tamari and lemon juice and continue cooking for 5 more minutes. Use as you would any barbecue sauce.

LINGUINI RED SAUCE

1 10-ounce can organic crushed tomatoes, or 3 ripe tomatoes,
  chopped

3 soy sausages, crumbled

½ teaspoon oregano

2 teaspoons Sucanat sweetener or raw sugar

½ teaspoon rosemary

2 tablespoons safflower oil

Heat the oil in a medium frying pan. Lightly brown the soy
sausage, then add the rest of the ingredients and bring to a boil.
Reduce heat to medium low and cook for 5 minutes. Serve on
top of cooked linguini or other pasta.

SPAGHETTI SAUCE

1 cup TVP granules (texturized vegetable protein)

1 16-ounce can crushed tomatoes

5 mushrooms, washed and sliced

1 tablespoon oregano

1 tablespoon Italian seasoning

1 tablespoon basil

1 teaspoon Sucanat® sweetener or ¼ teaspoon stevia

1 tablespoon vegetable broth powder

½ teaspoon salt (optional)

soy parmesan cheese as garnish (optional)

Soak the TVP in 2 cups of hot water for 5 minutes to soften it, then drain.

In a large saucepan, bring all ingredients (except cheese) to a boil, then reduce heat and simmer for 5 minutes. Serve over spaghetti with a fresh green salad. Garnish with soy parmesan cheese.

TOFU HOLLANDAISE SAUCE

10 ounces soft tofu

4 teaspoons plain nonfat yogurt

2 tablespoons yellow mustard

1 tablespoon lemon juice

1 tablespoon raw sugar or honey

2 dashes white pepper

dash cayenne pepper

Place all ingredients in blender and whip until smooth and creamy. Gently heat sauce until evenly hot and serve immediately over vegetables of your choice.

GUACAMOLE DIP

3 medium ripe avocados, peeled and mashed

1 medium ripe tomato, finely chopped

½ teaspoon chili powder

2 tablespoons lemon juice

¾ teaspoon real salt

In a large bowl, thoroughly mix all ingredients. Serve with organic corn chips or use as a sandwich spread.

TOFU DIP

2 cups soft tofu

⅓ cup oil

¼ cup vinegar

2 tablespoons nutritional yeast (optional)

1 tablespoon raw sugar

½ teaspoon real salt

1½ teaspoons soy sauce

Blend all ingredients to creamy consistency. Garnish with fresh, chopped dill or fresh peppermint leaves.

TOFU SOUR CREAM

1 cup tofu

½ cup oil

2 tablespoons lemon juice

1 teaspoon raw sugar (optional)

Thoroughly blend all ingredients. Use as mayonnaise or sour cream substitute.

Rice and Noodles

BROWN RICE

1 cup brown rice

3 cups water

Put the rice in a large, heavy saucepan and pour the water over it. Cover and bring to a boil at high heat.

Boil for 10 minutes, then reduce heat to low and simmer for 30 to 40 minutes, or until rice is tender. Do not stir the rice or it will become gummy.

If rice is soaked overnight (or all day), reduce simmering time to 20 minutes or less.

Makes about 2½ cups cooked rice or 2 servings

BROWN RICE WITH ADUKI BEANS

1 cup brown rice

1 15-ounce can aduki beans

1 piece kombu seaweed (3 to 6 inches long)

4 cups water

real salt to taste

Put the rice and water in a large saucepan and cook on high heat until boiling. Stir rice well, cover, reduce heat to medium low, and cook for another 45 minutes.

Stir in aduki beans and seaweed and cook for about 5 more minutes.

2 servings

BROWN RICE WITH CUMIN

1 cup brown rice

3 cups water

1 teaspoon ground cumin

1 tablespoon miso

1 bay leaf

2 tablespoons oil

½ cup water

Cook the brown rice in 3 cups water as directed in the "Brown Rice" recipe.

In a small bowl, combine the cumin, miso, bay leaf, and oil in ½ cup water. Add this mixture to the cooked rice and stir gently. Steam the covered rice for another 7 minutes; add a little more water if the rice is dry or not tender enough.

2 servings

BROWN RICE WITH LENTILS

½ cup lentils

1 cup brown rice

1 teaspoon ground coriander

⅓ teaspoon turmeric

2 tablespoons oil

1 dash cumin seeds

4 cups water

In a large saucepan, combine water, lentils, and rice and boil for 5 minutes. Reduce heat, add remaining ingredients, and simmer for 40 minutes more.

2 servings

BROWN RICE WITH YAMS

1 cup brown rice

1 medium yam, peeled and cubed

3 cups water

1 teaspoon finely grated fresh ginger

1 tablespoon miso

1 tablespoon oil

Soak the rice overnight (or all day) in 2 cups of water, then drain.

Place the rice, yams, and 3 cups fresh water in a heavy covered saucepan and bring to a boil. Reduce heat to medium low and cook for about 30 minutes or until rice and yams are tender. Dissolve the miso in a little warm water, then add miso, ginger, and oil to the rice pot and simmer for 15 minutes more. This is a great dish for cold winter days.

2 servings

FRIED RICE

3 cups cooked brown rice, refrigerated overnight

1 small carrot, cut in matchsticks

½ cup mixture of frozen peas and corn

½ cup vegetarian ham, cut in matchsticks

1 teaspoon dried marinated cabbage

3 tablespoons oil

½ teaspoon instant gravy

1 tablespoon pine nuts

1 tablespoon nori

1 tablespoon soy sauce

pinch of real salt

pinch of pepper

1 tablespoon canola margarine

Sitr-fry the carrots, peas, corn, and cabbage in the oil. Add rice, instant gravy, pine nuts, nori, soy sauce, salt and pepper, and mix it all together. Melt the margarine and drizzle it over the fried rice.

4 servings

ROASTED RICE SOUP

¾ cup brown or white rice

4 cups water

¼ teaspoon real salt

Toast the rice (without oil) in a frying pan until it turns golden brown. Add the water, bring to a boil, and simmer on medium-low heat for 45 minutes, if using white rice, or 60 to 90 minutes if using brown rice. Add more water if needed to maintain a soup consistency. Add salt and serve.

When you're ill, eat this soup 4 or 5 times throughout the day to ease symptoms of diarrhea, replenish fluids, and help restore energy.

2 servings

SUSHI

2½ cups cooked brown rice

4 pieces of seaweed sheet, about 12" × 4" each

1 small cucumber cut into thin 2–3 inch strips

6 soy sausage links

2 tablespoons vegenaise

1 tablespoon high-energy sesame mix

chopped coriander for garnish

Grill the soy links, remove from heat, and mash them with vegenaise. Stir in high-energy sesame mix and set aside.

To prepare each seaweed sheet, spread on ¼ of the rice, making sure to leave about ½ inch at end nearest you, ¼ inch along sides, and 1 inch at the farthest end. The rice will spread out as you roll the sheet; if rice is too sticky, dip your spoon or fingers in salt water for easier spreading.

Spread ¼ of the soy links on the top of the rice and sprinkle with a little coriander. Put a few strips of cucumber on the end nearest you and begin rolling away from you, making sure your hands are dry. A sushi mat helps make for compact rolling.

Hearty eaters can simply take the whole roll in hand, dip it in soy or wasabi sauce, and enjoy. For smaller, more dainty mouthfuls, cut the rolled sushi into ¾-inch slices and serve with sauce of your choice.

SWEET RICE

2 cups sweet rice

2 cups water

1 teaspoon sesame seeds

1 5-inch piece kombu seaweed, soaked (optional)

In a large saucepan, bring water to a boil and add rice. Return to boil and stir slowly until mixture becomes heavy. Cover and reduce heat to medium low. Cook another 10 to 15 minutes, adding soaked kombu if desired. Add sesame seeds, stir, and continue cooking for 3 more minutes or until rice is completely done.

2 servings

Note: Sweet rice is very easily digested and is well suited for weak and sick people. However, it cooks differently than other rice and needs getting used to. It becomes very sticky and can burn easily, so watch it carefully the first few times you cook it.

TOFU FRIED RICE

1 cup firm tofu, patted as dry as possible, and cubed

3 cups cooked brown or white rice

1 cup green peas

2 stalks thinly sliced celery

1 tablespoon coarsely grated carrot

2 tablespoons tamari

3 tablespoons oil

2 tablespoons water

cinnamon or mint leaves for garnish

In a large skillet, heat oil, water, and 1 tablespoon tamari. Stir-fry peas, celery, carrot, and tofu until lightly cooked. Add rice and 1 more tablespoon of tamari, reduce heat, and toss together until heated through. Garnish with a little cinnamon or mint leaves.

5 servings

WHITE RICE/BASMATI RICE

2 cups white rice or basmati rice, washed

4 cups water

In a large saucepan, combine rice and water. Bring to a boil for 5 minutes. Cover, reduce heat to medium low, and simmer for 15 minutes.

4 servings

STIR-FRIED RICE OR WHEAT NOODLES

5 cups cooked rice noodles or 5 cups cooked wheat noodles

½ cup carrot, coarsely chopped

½ cup celery, cut in thin strips

½ cup cabbage, cut in thin strips

5 fresh mushrooms, sliced

1 cup bean sprouts

½ pound wheat chicken, cut in thin strips

1 cup water

3 tablespoons canola oil

1 tablespoon vegetable broth

1 tablespoon tamari

2 tablespoons stir-fry sauce

dash of real salt

crushed roasted peanuts for garnish

fresh coriander or cilantro, finely chopped

Prepare the noodles by submerging them in hot water for 15 minutes; drain and set aside.

Heat a large frying pan to medium-high heat, add oil to hot pan, then add all other ingredients except noodles. Stir-fry evenly for 5 to 7 minutes; stir in noodles, mix well, and cook for another 3 to 5 minutes.

Serve on a platter, garnished with crushed roasted peanuts and coriander or cilantro.

6 servings

STIR-FRIED SOBA NOODLES

16 ounces soba noodles

5 dried black mushrooms, soaked and sliced

5 fresh mushrooms, sliced

1 cup bean sprouts

1 cup cabbage, sliced

½ cup baby corn

4 tablespoons safflower oil

2 tablespoons tamari

2 cups water

real salt and pepper to taste

fresh coriander or cilantro

Prepare the noodles by submerging them in hot water for 15 minutes. Drain and set aside.

Heat a large frying pan to medium heat, add oil, and stir in all vegetables and seasonings. Add water and cook for 7 minutes.

Mix noodles into stir-fry and cook for another 3 minutes. Garnish with cilantro.

4 servings

Tofu, Tempeh, and Seitan

ASPARAGUS & TOFU

1 pound asparagus, cut in 2-inch pieces

2 ounces tofu, cubed

½ cup water

1 tablespoon tamari

2 tablespoons sesame oil

1 tablespoon nutritional yeast (optional)

pinch of real salt

Combine all ingredients except oil in a skillet and cook at medium heat for 5 minutes or until asparagus is done but not soft. Mix in oil and heat for another minute; serve over rice or noodles.

Serves 4

BAKED TOFU WITH GREEN BEANS

½ pound green beans, cut in 1½-inch pieces

1 cup baked tofu, cubed

½ cup water

1 tablespoon canola oil

1 tablespoon soy sauce or tamari sauce

dash black pepper

¼ cup fresh cilantro for garnish

To bake the tofu, preheat oven to 350 degrees. Place ½-inch-thick slices of tofu on a baking sheet and bake them for 20 minutes or until tofu is golden yellow in color.

In a large skillet, heat water to boiling, then add beans and tofu. Stir-cook for 10 minutes, add tamari, pepper, and oil, and cook another 2 minutes (beans should be done but still crunchy).

Garnish with cilantro and serve with rice or potatoes.

Serves 4

BEAN SPROUT TOFU

2 cups bean sprouts

½ pound firm tofu

1 tablespoon tamari or soy sauce

1 tablespoon nutritional yeast

1 tablespoon chopped coriander

pinch of black pepper

½ cup canola oil for frying

1 tablespoon canola oil for stir-fry

Wash bean sprouts and remove the ends. Cut tofu in bite-size pieces and fry until golden brown. Drain fried tofu on paper towel.

Pour the used oil out of the frying pan, and reheat it at high heat with a tablespoon of fresh oil. Add the bean sprouts, fried tofu, soy sauce, and yeast. Stir-fry for 3 minutes.

Garnish with coriander and black pepper. For a complete meal, serve with soup and rice.

Serves 4

CAULIFLOW

¼ pound tofu

½ pound cauliflower, cut in bite-si

1 small carrot, thinly sliced

3 shiitake mushrooms

2 cups water

1 tablespoon tamari or soy sauce

1 tablespoon nutritional yeast

½ teaspoon raw sugar

1 tablespoon canola oil

1 tablespoon fresh chopped coriander

pinch of black pepper

Soak the mushrooms in a little hot water; then quarter them and save the soaking water.

Boil 2 cups fresh water and add cauliflower. Boil until pieces are tender and drain.

Tofu can be deep-fried (see "Bean Sprout Tofu" recipe) or cut in bite-size pieces and stir-fried with the rest of the ingredients.

Heat frying pan at high heat and add oil. Add tofu (deep-fried or raw), cauliflower, carrots, mushrooms and their soaking liquid, tamari, yeast, and sugar. Stir-fry for 5 minutes.

Garnish with coriander and black pepper and serve with rice or noodles.

Serves 4

COTTAGE TOFU

1 pound soft tofu, mashed

2 teaspoons apple cider or vinegar

2 teaspoons lemon juice

2 teaspoons canola oil

1 teaspoon real salt

choice of herbs (rosemary, thyme, parsley) to taste

black pepper

Mix together liquids, then add salt, pepper, and herbs. Add to mashed tofu. Chill and serve.

4 servings

CURRY TOFU

1 pound tofu, cubed

½ pound mushrooms, halved

2 sweet potatoes, cubed

1 pound white potatoes, cubed

2 16-ounce cans vegetable broth

1 16-ounce can coconut milk

2 8-inch stalks dried bean curd

1 cup deep-fried bean curd

2 large chopped green chilies of your choice

1 tablespoon curry powder

2 tablespoons finely chopped lemongrass

2 tablespoons canola oil

2 bay leaves

Soak the bean curd overnight (or all day), cut it in 1-inch pieces, and set aside.

Heat the oil in a large skillet; add lemongrass and sauté until golden brown. Stir in chopped chilies and curry powder and add ¼ can coconut milk to soften mixture. Add sweet potatoes, white potatoes, and soaked bean curd. Slowly stir in vegetable broth until all ingredients are well mixed.

Add bay leaves, cover, and cook for 15 minutes or until potatoes are just about done. Add fried bean curd, mushrooms, tofu, and remaining coconut milk. Cover and cook for another 5 minutes without lifting the lid. Serve with rice noodles, rice, or bread.

Serves 6

MUSHROOM AND LILY STUFFED TOFU

1 pound tofu, cut in four thick slices and baked

5 pieces dried black fungus

6 dried shiitake mushrooms

1½-ounce package bean thread

15 dried lilies

5 ripe tomatoes

1 tablespoon nutritional yeast

1 tablespoon canola oil

2 tablespoons tamari

1 teaspoon raw sugar

real salt and pepper to taste

fresh parsley for garnish

Preheat oven to 350 degrees; place four slices of tofu on baking sheet and bake for 20 minutes or until tofu is golden yellow in color.

Soak fungus, mushrooms, bean thread, and lilies separately in hot water for 5 minutes, drain, and pat dry. Chop all the soaked ingredients finely and combine them in a bowl; set aside.

Peel, seed, and finely chop tomatoes. Heat oil in a skillet and cook tomatoes with tamari for 7 minutes at low heat.

Slice baked tofu pieces along one edge and scoop some tofu out to form a pocket. Combine extracted tofu with mushroom mixture and stuff into pockets. Place stuffed tofu in skillet with the tomato sauce, bring to a boil, and immediately remove from heat. Serve over rice garnished with parsley.

Serves 4

SPICY LEMONGRASS TOFU

1 pound tofu, cut in 1½-inch cubes

3 stalks celery, cut in ½-inch diagonal slices

1 tablespoon chopped lemongrass

1 teaspoon curry powder

2 tablespoons raw sugar

½ teaspoon five spices

½ teaspoon red chilies (optional)

1 tablespoon soy sauce or tamari

canola oil

Deep-fry the tofu cubes until they are golden brown; set aside.

Warm a skillet to medium-high heat, then add 2 tablespoons of oil to warm it. Add all ingredients except celery and stir-cook until everything is well mixed. Add celery, cover, lower the heat, and cook for 5 more minutes. Serve over rice.

Serves 4

STEAMED TOFU DELICACY

¾ pound tofu, mashed

1½ ounce package bean thread noodles

6 dried shiitake mushrooms

6 pieces black fungus

8 1-inch chao cubes

3 8-inch square sheets dried bean curd (paper thin)

¼ teaspoon black pepper

½ teaspoon Sucanat sweetener or raw sugar

1 tablespoon nutritional yeast

4 tablespoons tapioca flour (reserve 2 tablespoons for sauce)

2 tablespoons ketchup

Pour hot water over bean thread and soak it for 15 minutes; drain, dry on paper towels, then chop into small pieces. Prepare the mushrooms and the fungus the same way.

In a large bowl, thoroughly mix together all ingredients except ketchup and 2 tablespoons of tapioca flour; then divide mixture into 3 heat-proof ceramic bowls.

Arrange the 3 bowls in a large pot with a lid and enough water to steam them for 30 minutes. You can put them on a strong steamer tray or basket or else just be sure the water doesn't leak into the bowls. Cover and steam for 30 minutes.

For sauce, mix together the ketchup and reserved tapioca flour. Spread on top of the steamed bowls (being careful not to burn yourself), cover, and steam for 8 more minutes.

Serves 4

STIR-FRY MUSHROOMS AND TOFU

1 pound mushrooms, quartered

½ pound firm tofu, cut in bite-size pieces

3 stalks celery, cut diagonally in thin slices

1 tablespoon tamari or soy sauce

1 tablespoon nutritional yeast

1 tablespoon fresh chopped coriander

pinch of black pepper

½ cup canola oil for frying

1 tablespoon canola oil for stir-frying

Heat oil in a wok or heavy frying pan at high heat. Fry the tofu until golden brown and drain on paper towel.

Remove frying oil from pan and heat a fresh tablespoon of oil at high heat. Add fried tofu, mushrooms, celery, tamari, and yeast. Stir-fry for 5 minutes.

Garnish with coriander and pepper. Serve with rice and soup or salad for a meal.

Serves 4

STUFFED TOFU LEMONGRASS

1 pound firm tofu

2 tablespoons lemongrass, finely chopped

1 tablespoon sesame seeds

¼ teaspoon real salt

⅛ teaspoon black pepper

1 tablespoon Sucanat sweetener or raw sugar

1 teaspoon instant gravy

1 tablespoon nutritional yeast

1 tablespoon tamari sauce

3 tablespoons canola oil

Mix together all ingredients except the tofu and mash into a nice uniform paste.

Pat dry the tofu and cut into 8 slices (about 1-inch thick). Cut open one edge of each tofu piece to make a pocket; stuff the lemongrass paste into the tofu pockets. Fry the tofu on both sides until golden brown. (It works well to stuff the tofu, refrigerate it for up to 8 hours, then fry it.) Serve with rice.

4 servings

SWEET PEAS WITH TOFU

1 pound sweet peas

¼ pound firm tofu, cubed

½ cup water

1 tablespoon oil

½ teaspoon sweet basil

soy sauce to taste

Warm the oil in a large skillet and sauté all ingredients for about 4 minutes. Serve over rice.

Serves 4

TOFU AND SPINACH
STUFFED MUSHROOMS

1 10-ounce package frozen spinach

24 very large fresh mushrooms

½ cup soft tofu, crumbled

¾ cup canola margarine

¾ cup fine bread crumbs

¼ teaspoon ground nutmeg

real salt and pepper to taste

Preheat oven to 350 degrees.

Cook spinach according to package instructions, drain well, and puree in blender.

Gently wash the mushrooms and pat dry; remove and finely chop the stems. Melt margarine at low heat in a medium saucepan; dip each mushroom cap, and place on oiled cookie sheet.

Add chopped mushroom stems and all other ingredients to the melted margarine and mix well. Fill each mushroom cap with stuffing and bake for 15 minutes. Serve with rice or potatoes and salad.

24 servings

TOFU SCRAMBLE

1 pound firm tofu, crumbled

5 fresh mushrooms, sliced

1 teaspoon oregano

1 teaspoon basil

2 teaspoons turmeric

2 teaspoons vegetable broth powder

2 teaspoons cumin (optional)

2 tablespoons safflower oil

pinch of real salt

chopped coriander and black pepper for garnish

Heat oil in frying pan, add all ingredients, stir well, and sauté for 5 minutes. Garnish with coriander and pepper and serve with bread or soy sausage. A great dish for breakfast, brunch, or a quick lunch.

Serves 4

TOFU WITH BOK CHOY

1 pound bok choy, cut in 1-inch pieces

½ pound baked tofu, cubed

1 tomato, quartered

½ cup water

1 teaspoon fresh ginger, finely chopped

1 tablespoon canola oil

dash of black pepper

tamari to taste

parsley to garnish

Preheat oven to 350 degrees. Place ½-inch-thick slices of tofu on baking sheet and bake for 20 minutes or until tofu is golden yellow in color. Then cube the tofu.

Heat the oil in a skillet, add all ingredients, and stir-fry for 5 minutes. Garnish with parsley and serve with potatoes or rice.

Serves 4

CHAYOTE WITH TEMPEH

2 chayotes, peeled, pitted, and cut in ¼-inch pieces

5 ounces tempeh, cut in ¼-inch pieces

1 cup water

1 teaspoon nutritional yeast

1 teaspoon safflower oil

soy sauce to taste

fresh cilantro or coriander to garnish

In a saucepan, boil water, chayote, tempeh, and soy sauce at medium heat for 10 minutes. Add yeast and oil and cook another 3 minutes.

Garnish with fresh herb and serve with rice and salad or soup.

Note: Chayote is a common Asian and South American food; it's called chocho in Brazil. It is a pear-shaped vegetable low in calories and rich in vitamins. It should not be eaten raw; peel it under cool running water and pit it before cooking.

Serves 4

INDONESIAN FRIED TEMPEH

¼ pound tempeh, cut in very thin slices

4 tablespoons warm water

1 teaspoon real salt

2 teaspoons turmeric

4 slices of lemon or lime

dash black pepper

dash saffron powder

canola oil for frying

Mix salt, pepper, saffron powder, and turmeric with warm water. Add tempeh slices to marinate them, then drain off liquid. Add oil to frying pan at medium high heat and fry tempeh until browned. Squeeze lemon or lime juice over tempeh and serve.

Serves 4

TEMPEH & FRESH MUSHROOMS

1½ cups tempeh, cubed

1½ cups fresh mushrooms, quartered

1 cup sweet peas (optional)

2 tablespoons water

1 tablespoon soy sauce or tamari

1 tablespoon canola oil

dash of curry, ginger, or chopped lemongrass

Heat the oil at medium-high heat in a large skillet; add all ingredients and stir-cook for 5 minutes or until done. Serve over brown rice.

Serves 4

BARBECUED SEITAN

1 pound seitan

½ cup oil

½ cup nutritional yeast

½ cup tahini or peanut butter

½ cup barbecue sauce
   (see recipe in "Salads, Dressings, and Sauces")

dash of real salt

Preheat oven to 350 degrees.

Pull seitan into strips with your fingers. In a mixing bowl, combine all other ingredients, coat each seitan strip, then let the strips sit on a plate for 10 minutes.

Place the coated strips on a well-oiled cookie sheet and bake for 15 minutes. Remove from oven and turn heat down to 250 degrees.

Brush top of the seitan strips with barbecue sauce, turn and brush other side of strips, then bake for 10 more minutes. Serve with rice, vegetables, and salad.

Serves 4

LEMONGRASS SEITAN

1 pound seitan

3 medium stalks lemongrass, finely chopped

2 teaspoons tamari

1 teaspoon raw sugar

1 teaspoon canola oil

Slice seitan in thin strips. Soak the strips in tamari and marinate them overnight (or all day) in the refrigerator. Before cooking, mix in the sugar and oil.

In a frying pan, cook the seitan and its sauce on medium-low heat for 10 minutes, stirring constantly. Add the lemongrass and cook for 5 more minutes, continuing to stir. Serve with rice or boiled potatoes and salad.

Serves 4

SEITAN WITH GRAVY

1 pound seitan, thinly sliced

1 stalk lemongrass, finely chopped

1 tablespoon oil

1 teaspoon instant gravy mix

1 teaspoon nutritional yeast

Sauté the lemongrass in the oil at medium-low heat for 3 minutes, then add seitan and cook for another 5 minutes. Season with instant gravy and nutritional yeast; add a little soy sauce if you like.

Serves 4

Vegetable Entrées and Side Dishes

ASPARAGUS AND SHIITAKE MUSHROOM SPLENDOR

2 cups asparagus, cut in 1½-inch pieces

1 small carrot, cut in 1½-inch strips

1 cup fresh shiitake mushrooms, cut in half, if large

2 tablespoons vegetarian stir-fry sauce

4 tablespoons water

1 teaspoon chopped or sliced ginger

high-energy sesame mix for garnish (see recipe in this section)

a little oil to brown the ginger

Brown the ginger in a skillet, then add asparagus. Carefully pour water around sides of skillet, then add carrots, mushrooms, and stir-fry sauce. Add a little more water if needed for steaming.

Cover, turn heat off, and steam for a few minutes; make sure vegetables keep some crunch. Serve immediately, garnished with high-energy sesame mix.

Serves 4

CHI BURGERS

2 cups uncooked instant oatmeal

⅔ cup uncooked cream of buckwheat

⅔ cup cooked brown rice

⅔ cup cooked sweet rice

⅔ cup cooked quinoa or soybeans

⅔ cup raw carrots, finely grated

2 tablespoons nutritional yeast

2 teaspoons lemongrass, finely chopped

1 teaspoon tamari

½ teaspoon real salt

½ teaspoon cumin

¼ teaspoon black pepper

In a large bowl, mix together all ingredients. Form mixture into patties. Fry in canola oil or freeze for later use.

Makes 6 to 8 patties.

CHICK PEAS & VEGETABLES

2 cups cooked chick peas (garbanzo beans)

1 carrot, thinly sliced

1 head broccoli florets

1 cup water

1 tablespoon oil

tamari to taste

1 teaspoon fresh chopped coriander

Bring the water to a boil in a skillet and add all ingredients. Stir-cook for about 10 minutes or a little less (so vegetables are still crunchy). Garnish with fresh coriander and serve over rice.

Serves 4

"CHICKEN" AND BLACK MUSHROOMS

½ pound wheat meat chicken, cut into bite-size pieces

6 black mushrooms, quartered

5 button mushrooms, quartered

2 sweet potatoes, peeled and cubed

2 tomatoes, cubed

16-ounce can of coconut milk

2 cups water

1 teaspoon instant gravy

2 teaspoons tamari

1 tablespoon oil

In a medium skillet, fry the wheat meat in oil for 5 minutes at high heat. Then bring all ingredients to a boil in a soup pot and simmer for 15 minutes. Serve with brown rice or whole grain bread.

Serves 6

CHILI

16-ounce can kidney beans

16-ounce can pinto beans

16-ounce can vegetarian baked beans

16-ounce can lima beans

16-ounce can peeled tomatoes, chopped

1 cup TVP granules (texturized vegetable protein)

3 sweet potatoes, peeled and cut in bite-size cubes

2 zucchini or 1 butternut squash, peeled and cut in bite-size cubes

12 fresh mushrooms, quartered

2 medium-size green chili peppers, chopped coarsely

3 tablespoons chili powder

½ teaspoon sugar

½ teaspoon instant gravy

2 cups water

Soak the TVP in 2 cups hot water for 5 minutes to soften it, then drain. In a soup pot, combine all ingredients and bring to a boil. Cook at medium heat for 30 minutes, stirring occasionally. Serve with rice. This dish is good the next day, too.

Serves 12

COCONUT "CHICKEN" KORMA

½ pound wheat meat chicken, cut in bite-size pieces

3 ripe tomatoes

4-ounce can tomato paste

16-ounce can coconut milk, divided into 2 bowls

2 cups water

2 tablespoons canola oil

4 inches ginger root, thinly sliced

2 tablespoons lemongrass, finely chopped

1 packet chicken korma seasoning

1 teaspoon vegetable broth powder

2 teaspoons tamari

½ teaspoon real salt

juice of 1 lemon or lime

5 tablespoons blanched almonds or roasted cashews

1 tablespoon fresh coriander

In a nonstick skillet sauté the wheat meat chicken on high heat with the ginger and lemongrass until golden brown. Sprinkle in the packet of seasoning and continue cooking until spice seeds begin to pop. Stir in chopped tomatoes, tomato paste, broth powder, tamari, and salt.

Mix water with ½ can of coconut milk; add to the "chicken" and stir for 5 minutes at medium heat. Turn heat off and cover for a minute or two. Add other half of coconut milk, bring to a boil again, and turn heat off immediately.

To serve, squeeze the fresh lemon or lime over the dish and garnish with nuts and coriander.

Serves 6

EGGLESS EGG ROLLS

egg roll wrappers (look for wrappers made without eggs)

2 cups canola oil for deep-frying

FILLING:

1 pound soft tofu

2 medium carrots, shredded

1 cup cabbage, shredded

5 ounces bean thread

5 shiitake mushrooms

1 tablespoon tamari

2 teaspoons raw sugar

2 tablespoons nutritional yeast

½ teaspoon black pepper

½ teaspoon real salt

SAUCE FOR EGGLESS EGG ROLLS:

½ cup shredded carrot

1 cup boiling water

1 tablespoon raw sugar

1 tablespoon tamari or soy sauce

2 teaspoons vinegar or lime juice

pinch of real salt

Crumble the tofu and pat it dry with paper towel. Soak bean thread in hot water for 10 minutes, drain, pat dry, and cut in thin strips. Wash bean sprouts and remove the ends. In a large bowl, combine all filling ingredients and seasonings.

For the dipping sauce, dissolve sugar in boiling water, then mix in all other sauce ingredients.

TO ASSEMBLE THE ROLLS:

Place wrappers on a flat surface; spread 2 tablespoons of filling on the top third of the wrapper, leaving enough of an edge at the top to fold over the filling. Fold the top edge over the filling, then fold the left and right sides of the wrapper over and roll the top (filled) portion away from you, forming an enclosed roll. Make sure you've encased all the filling in the folded and rolled wrapper so that the rolls won't leak during frying.

Heat the oil in a wok or heavy pot for deep-frying; the oil should be very hot but not smoking. Deep-fry the eggless egg rolls a few at a time until they are golden brown and crispy, making sure they are not crowded in the fryer. Drain fried rolls on paper towel.

Dip rolls in sauce and serve with lettuce and fresh coriander or basil.

This is a fun dish to make at family gatherings, with everybody pitching in to help prepare the rolls.

Makes 12 to 18 rolls

EGGPLANT CANTONESE

3 medium eggplants, sliced diagonally in ¼-inch slices

2 tablespoons soy sauce

3 drops sesame oil

dash black pepper

1 teaspoon pickled cabbage, thinly sliced
   (optional; see recipe in this section)

1 tablespoon canola oil for pan-frying

2 teaspoons high-energy sesame mix for garnish
   (see recipe in this section)

Mix the soy sauce, sesame oil, and pepper in a small bowl.

Heat a little oil on medium heat in a large non-stick frying pan.
Arrange a layer of eggplant slices in the pan, making sure they
don't overlap (you will need to cook more than one batch). Pour
some canola oil on a spoon and drip it on the eggplant in a clock-
wise direction, starting at the middle of the pan and moving in a
spiral toward the sides. Use enough oil to evenly brown the eggplant, turn the eggplant over, and repeat.

When the eggplant is grilled, add the soy sauce mixture and stir
in pickled cabbage. Garnish with high-energy sesame mix and
serve immediately over warm rice.

The preparation time for this dish is well worth the effort; pan-
frying eggplant is an art of its own. Listening to soft, soothing
music while you cook will quiet your mind and help you enjoy
your efforts.

Serves 4

GINGER WHEAT "CHICKEN"

½ pound wheat meat chicken, thinly sliced

2 cups baby carrots or daikon

1 tablespoon fresh ginger, thinly sliced

1 cup hot water

1 tablespoon tamari

½ teaspoon Sucanat sweetener or raw sugar

1 tablespoon sesame oil

Heat the oil in a frying pan and add all ingredients. Stir-cook at medium heat for 5 minutes. Cover and turn off stove. Let sit for 10 minutes. Good served with rice and soup.

Serves 4

GRILLED EGGPLANT

4 medium eggplants, quartered lengthwise

3 tablespoons soy sauce or tamari

2 drops stevia

1 teaspoon sesame oil

2 tablespoons ginger, finely chopped

canola oil sufficient to grill eggplant and fry ginger

coriander or cilantro to garnish

Mix the soy sauce, stevia, and sesame oil together in a small bowl. Fry the ginger in a little oil until golden brown and add to soy sauce mixture.

Drip oil onto the eggplant quarters, then grill them in a little oil until tender, turning to grill evenly. When eggplants are tender, stir in the sauce mix and heat through.

Serve immediately with garnish of your choice.

Serves 4

HIGH-ENERGY SESAME MIX

1 pound sesame seeds

2 teaspoons real salt

3 tablespoons nutritional yeast

In a non-stick frying pan, roast seeds with salt at medium-high heat (without oil) until seeds are golden brown. Stir constantly to prevent burning. Mix in nutritional yeast.

This is a versatile mix. Use it to season brown rice or other dishes, or sprinkle it on toast, salad, or vegetables. Store in a closed container to keep it fresh.

HOMEMADE CABBAGE PICKLES

1 medium cabbage, cut in large bite-size pieces

1 teaspoon real salt mixed in ¼ cup water

3 tablespoons apples cider vinegar

5 tablespoons Sucanat® sweetener or raw sugar

1 teaspoon real salt

your choice of red peppers, carrots, dill, or other herbs

Soak the cabbage pieces in salted water for 2 days. Drain and squeeze water out of cabbage.

In a large bowl, mix together the vinegar, Sucanat, and salt, then add the cabbage and stir. For extra spice, add red peppers, dill, or herbs of your choice. Add some sliced or grated carrot for color and crunch.

This is a versatile relish which can be added to other dishes, used as a side dish, or spread on sandwiches. Keeps under refrigeration for up to a month.

INDIAN DAHL

2 cups uncooked yellow split peas

8 cups water

1½ cups kale or spinach, coarsely chopped

2 tablespoons canola oil

1 tablespoon fresh ginger root, peeled and finely chopped

1 teaspoon real salt

¼ teaspoon ground cumin

¼ teaspoon turmeric

⅛ teaspoon cayenne pepper

In a large covered pot, cook split peas in water for 45 minutes at medium heat; mix in all other ingredients and continue cooking for 30 more minutes.

MACHIG'S STEW

5 cups water

1 cup seitan or vegetarian wheat meatballs

2 medium eggplants, cut in 1-inch cubes

1 cup pineapple pieces (fresh or canned), cut in 1-inch cubes

2 cups tomatoes, cut in 1-inch cubes

10 shiitake mushrooms, soaked and quartered

½ cup bamboo shoots (optional)

1 teaspoon soy sauce

1 teaspoon vegetarian oyster sauce or Sucanat sweetener

1 teaspoon vegetable broth powder

1 teaspoon oil

1 teaspoon nutritional yeast

Bring water to a boil in a stockpot. Add the seitan (or wheat balls), eggplant, pineapple, tomatoes, mushrooms, and bamboo shoots. Then add soy sauce, oyster sauce (or Sucanat), broth powder, oil, and nutritional yeast.

Bring to a boil again, then turn down heat to medium low. Cover and let simmer for 10 to 15 minutes. Serve with rice.

Serves 6

MUSHROOM PICKLE

1 pound fresh mushrooms

⅔ cup vinegar

⅔ cup raw sugar

1 tablespoon canola oil

2 teaspoons real salt

Wash the mushrooms and put them in boiling water for 3 minutes. Drain. Mix other ingredients together in a large lidded jar and add mushrooms. Cover the jar and let it sit unrefrigerated for 2 days. Once open, pickles keep up to a month in the refrigerator.

OKRA MASALA

½ pound okra, cut in 1-inch lengths

¼ pound cauliflower, cut in bite-size pieces

1 medium carrot, cut in 1-inch lengths

2 tomatoes, chopped

1 cup frozen peas

1 thumb-size piece ginger root, finely chopped

3 stalks lemongrass, finely chopped

2 cups water

1 tablespoon canola oil

1 cup plain yogurt or coconut milk

1 packet vegetable masala seasoning

1 tablespoon nutritional yeast

1 teaspoon vegetable broth powder

real salt and pepper to taste

chopped coriander or cilantro for garnish

Bring water to boil in a saucepan and add salt, carrots, and cauliflower; cover and turn off heat.

In a non-stick frying pan, heat oil and sauté ginger and lemongrass until golden brown; then add seasoning packet and fry until fragrant. Stir in tomatoes and okra, then pour boiled ingredients and their stock into okra mixture and add peas.

Mix in yeast, vegetable broth powder, and salt and pepper; cover and simmer for 5 to 10 minutes. When okra is tender, stir in yogurt or coconut milk. Cover and simmer another 5 minutes. Serve over rice or noodles, garnished with coriander or cilantro.

You can substitute a vegetable of your choice for the okra if you want to vary this recipe.

Serves 4

SEAWEED WITH GREEN VEGETABLES

1 10-inch piece of kombu seaweed

10 medium mushrooms, quartered

½ pound snow peas or sweet peas

5 stalks asparagus, cut in 2-inch pieces

1 medium carrot, cut in 2-inch pieces

1 small green pepper, cut in bite-size pieces

1 tablespoon canola oil

1 tablespoon tamari

4 cups water

Soak kombu for 5 minutes and cut in 1-inch squares. In a soup pot, boil kombu and carrot in water for 5 minutes. Add remaining ingredients and boil at medium heat for 15 minutes. Good served with brown rice and soup.

Serves 4

SOYBEAN PATTIES

2 cups dried soybeans

⅔ cup whole wheat or teff flour

⅓ cup wheat germ

¼ cup tamari

1 tablespoon parsley, chopped

½ teaspoon basil

½ teaspoon thyme

½ teaspoon celery seed

4 cups water from cooked soybeans

¼ to ½ cup oil

real salt to taste

Cover soybeans with plenty of water and soak them overnight (or all day). Drain them and boil in 5 cups fresh water for 45 minutes, until they are soft.

In a blender or food processor, thoroughly blend the cooked beans. In a large bowl, mix the soybean paste with all other ingredients and form mixture into patties.

Heat the oil in a large frying pan and fry patties until golden brown. Serve them on top of green leafy salad or make sandwiches.

Serves 6

SPICED CHICK PEAS

MASALA SEASONING MIXTURE:

1 teaspoon ground black pepper

1 teaspoon red chili

½ teaspoon real salt

1 teaspoon cumin powder

3 teaspoons mango powder

Mix spices together and store in an airtight container. You can also buy masala spice mixture at an Indian grocery store.

CHICK PEA MIXTURE:

2 16-ounce cans chick peas (garbanzo beans)

2 medium tomatoes, peeled, seeded, and coarsely chopped

1 tablespoon fresh ginger, finely chopped

1 teaspoon curry powder

1 teaspoon masala seasoning mix

2 tablespoons peanut oil

1 teaspoon tamari

8 drops hot sauce or ⅛ teaspoon chili powder

In a bowl, blend tomatoes with curry, ginger, and masala spice mixture.

Heat the oil in a skillet and sauté the tomato mixture with tamari until golden brown. Lower heat and mash mixture with back of spoon to form a paste.

Add chick peas and ½ cup of the liquid to the paste and cook for 5 minutes. Add hot sauce to taste. If you prefer, you can lightly blend the chick pea mixture before serving. Good with brown rice.

Serves 4

SPINACH LASAGNA

1 box lasagna noodles

1 box frozen chopped spinach, thawed

1 pound tofu, crumbled

16-ounce can crushed tomatoes

½ teaspoon real salt

½ teaspoon pepper

1 green pepper, diced

6 stalks celery, diced

2 to 3 tomatoes, diced

1½ teaspoons dried parsley

1½ teaspoons dried basil

1½ teaspoons dried oregano

16 ounces soy parmesan cheese, grated

Preheat oven to 350 degrees.

Cook the noodles in a large pot; drain, rinse, and set aside.

In a large mixing bowl, combine all ingredients except parmesan cheese. Layer noodles and filling in a lightly oiled large baking pan, starting with a layer of noodles and ending with a layer of the filling. Cover with parmesan cheese and pour ½ cup of water over the lasagna. Bake for 45 minutes or until done all the way through.

Serves 6

SWEET & SOUR PINEAPPLE

BASIC INGREDIENTS:

1 cup fresh pineapple, diced

1 ripe tomato, quartered

1 cup seitan, cut in bite-size pieces

½ cup green pepper, cut in thin strips

½ cup mushrooms, sliced

½ cup water

1 tablespoon canola oil

THICKENING MIXTURE:

1 teaspoon tapioca powder

1 cup water

1 tablespoon vinegar

1 tablespoon raw sugar

1 tablespoon soy sauce or tamari

Combine basic ingredients in a medium-size pot and cook on medium heat for 3 to 4 minutes.

In a small bowl, mix the thickening ingredients together and add them to the pot, stirring well. Reduce heat to low and cook for another 3 minutes. Garnish with your favorite herb and serve over rice.

Serves 4

STUFFED MUSHROOMS

12 large mushrooms with stems removed
  (keep them)

½ cup firm tofu, crumbled

½ cup bread crumbs

3 teaspoons canola oil

1 tablespoon nutritional yeast

½ teaspoon thyme

1 teaspoon tamari

dash real salt

Preheat oven to 350 degrees.

Finely chop the mushroom stems and mix them in a bowl with all other ingredients except mushroom caps. Stuff mixture into caps and bake on an oiled cookie sheet for 15 minutes.

Serves 4

TASTY BROCCOLI WITH
MUSHROOM SAUCE

3 cups broccoli, cut in bite-size pieces

½ cup water

2 tablespoons vegetarian mushroom sauce

1 teaspoon ginger, sliced or chopped

1 tablespoon canola oil

1 teaspoon nutritional yeast

pinch of real salt

dash of black pepper

pinch of high-energy sesame mix
  (optional: see recipe in this section)

Bring water to a boil in a saucepan. Add broccoli and cover. Turn heat off and set aside; do not lift cover until you're ready to add to the sauce.

Heat the oil in a skillet and stir-fry ginger until golden brown. Add mushroom sauce, broccoli, and broccoli stock and mix well. Sprinkle in salt, pepper, yeast, and high-energy mix and serve with rice or noodles. This is a quick, tasty dish after a hectic day.

Serves 4

VEGETABLE PROTEIN LOAF

1 pound TVP granules (texturized vegetable protein)

⅔ cup egg substitute

½ cup bread crumbs

⅓ cup soy milk or rice milk

¼ cup celery, finely chopped

¼ cup fresh parsley, finely chopped

½ teaspoon real salt

½ teaspoon vegetable broth powder

¼ teaspoon black pepper

dash of sage

dash of nutmeg

Preheat oven to 350 degrees.

Mix all ingredients together in a large bowl and pat into lightly oiled meatloaf pan. Cover with foil and bake for 35 minutes. Remove cover, brush top with egg substitute, turn oven off, and return pan to oven for another 10 minutes.

Serves 6

VEGETARIAN "LAMB" CHUNK DELICACY

7-ounce package vegetarian lamb chunks

3 red potatoes, cut in pieces

6 fresh mushrooms, quartered

2 carrots, quartered and cut in 2-inch pieces

2 cups water

1 tablespoon tomato paste

1 tablespoon vegetarian stir-fry sauce

1 teaspoon vegetable broth powder

1 teaspoon curry powder

1 tablespoon lemongrass, finely chopped

1 tablespoon canola oil

coriander to garnish

Heat the oil in a large frying pan and sauté lemongrass until golden brown. Combine remaining ingredients in the frying pan, bring to a boil, then reduce heat to low. Cover and simmer for 15 minutes. Garnish with fresh coriander and serve with bread or rice.

Serves 4

VEGETARIAN LASAGNA

1 package lasagna noodles

4 cups crushed tomatoes

3 cups tomato sauce

1 cup tomato paste

1 veggie burger, cut in small pieces

1 10-ounce package frozen chopped spinach, thawed

16 ounces soft tofu or soy cheese, crumbled

1 cup mushrooms, sliced

½ cup bread crumbs

¼ cup olive oil

¾ teaspoons real salt

1½ teaspoons dried parsley

1½ teaspoons basil

1½ teaspoons oregano

1 tablespoon raw sugar

1 tablespoon tamari

Preheat oven to 350 degrees.

In a large pot, boil the noodles according to package instructions; drain, rinse, and set aside.

In a large bowl, combine all other ingredients and mix well.

Lightly oil a baking pan, and alternate layers of noodles and filling, ending with a layer of filling. Pour ½ cup water over the top, cover, and bake for 30 minutes or until hot all the way through. Leftovers make great lunches!

VEGETARIAN PIZZA

CRUST:

¾ cup water

½ cup whole wheat flour

1 cup oat flour

Mix crust ingredients well to form a dough and press into oiled pie plate. Place in steamer or double boiler for 15 minutes at medium heat; remove from steamer and let cool. (You can also use ready-made whole wheat pastry crust from your grocery or natural food store and omit the steaming process.)

TOPPING:

4 tofu or soy wieners, thinly sliced

½ cup green pepper, finely chopped

⅓ cup red pepper, finely chopped

1 small avocado, peeled, pitted,
   and thinly sliced

3 button mushrooms, chopped

3 black olives, finely chopped

8 ounces grated soy cheese
   or crumbled soft tofu

8-ounce can crushed tomatoes

⅓ cup natural ketchup

½ teaspoon rosemary

½ teaspoon oregano

Preheat oven to 375 degrees.

Mix tomatoes, ketchup, rosemary, and oregano together in a bowl. Spread mixture on the pizza crust, then cover with half the cheese or tofu. Place the wieners, peppers, avocado, mushrooms, and olives over the top of the pizza, then sprinkle with the remaining cheese or tofu. Bake for 35 minutes.

Serves 4

VIETNAMESE CURRY

½ pound firm tofu, cubed

2 small red potatoes, thickly cubed

2 sweet potatoes, thickly cubed

2 carrots, thickly sliced

5 fresh shiitake mushrooms, halved

8 cups water

canola oil

Sucanat sweetener or raw sugar

real salt

turmeric

cumin

curry powder

instant vegetarian gravy mix

12 ounces canned coconut milk

Sauté tofu until golden brown and drain on paper towel. Then sauté potatoes and carrots with a little salt, Sucanat, and curry powder.

In a large pot, bring water to a boil and add tofu, sautéed potatoes and carrots, and mushrooms. Cook at medium heat for 20 minutes. Add more salt, Sucanat, and curry powder, along with instant gravy, turmeric, and cumin to taste. Cook for a few more minutes until tastes are well blended to your liking.

Carefully remove about 2 cups' worth of the potatoes and carrots and mash them in a bowl. Add this mixture back into the pot and continue cooking for 5 more minutes. Add the coconut milk, bring to a boil, and remove from heat. Serve with rice noodles.

Serves 6

ZUCCHINI AND EGGPLANT COMBO

1 pound zucchini, cut in ⅛-inch slices

1 medium eggplant, peeled and cut in ⅛-inch slices

1 pound tomatoes, peeled and finely chopped

2 teaspoons tamari

1 teaspoon basil

1 tablespoon oregano

1 teaspoon raw sugar

3 teaspoons canola oil

real salt to taste

In a large skillet, sauté tomatoes, basil, oregano, and sugar in one teaspoon oil for 3 minutes, then put mixture in a bowl and set aside.

Add 2 more teaspoons oil to frying pan and sauté zucchini and eggplant with tamari for 8 minutes or until evenly done. Add tomato mixture back to pan and cook for 10 more minutes. Serve with rice.

Serves 6

Beverages and Desserts

BANANA SESAME AMAZAKE DRINK

1 cup plain amazake

1 tablespoon sesame tahini

1 ripe banana

½ cup water

Blend all ingredients well in a blender. You can drink it right away or chill first.

1 serving

BANANA SMOOTHIE

1 cup soy milk

1 cup ice

3 medium ripe bananas

2 tablespoons raw sugar or honey

dash real salt

Blend all ingredients in a blender and serve immediately.

1 to 2 servings

GINGER AMAZAKE TEA

2 cups plain amazake

1½ cups water

½ to 1 teaspoon finely grated ginger

Bring amazake and water to boil. Remove from heat and stir in ginger. Serve in tea cups. This is a traditional Japanese drink that is very soothing.

2 to 3 servings

GINGER TEA

thumb-size piece of ginger root

4 cups water

Peel the ginger, cut into thin slices, and add to boiling water. Turn heat to low for 10 minutes.

Add maple syrup, stevia, honey, or black strap molasses to sweeten the tea if you like.

Drink 3 or 4 cups a day for the tea's restorative effect.

4 servings

HOMEMADE SOY MILK

2½ cups organic soybeans

2½ cups hot water

raw sugar to taste

Soak beans overnight (or all day) in refrigerator in 5 cups water. After soaking, rinse them well and place in blender with fresh hot water. Blend at high speed until beans are well ground.

Pour into heavy-bottomed pot and bring to a boil. Immediately reduce heat to low and simmer for 20 minutes, stirring constantly to avoid burning or boiling over.

Strain through cheesecloth or cotton linen. Add sugar if you wish; drink as is or use in other recipes.

4 servings

SOY NOG

3 cups soy milk

½ cup raw sugar

1 teaspoon natural vanilla

1 tablespoon canola oil

dash nutmeg

Put everything in a blender and blend well. Serve warm or cold.

3 servings

AMAZAKE GELATIN DESSERT

1 cup amazake (any flavor)

1 tablespoon agar-agar flakes (see vegetable gelatin)

In a small saucepan, bring the ingredients to a boil while stirring constantly. Reduce heat and simmer 5 minutes or until gelatin is dissolved. Pour into serving dish and chill until firm.

1 serving

BLUEBERRY ALMOND MOUSSE

1 cup soy milk

1 quart unsweetened apple juice

2 12-inch × 1-inch bars agar-agar, cut in 1-inch pieces

1 teaspoon vanilla extract

1 teaspoon lemon juice

4 teaspoons almond butter

1 cup blueberries

3 teaspoons pure maple syrup

¼ cup toasted almond slivers

Combine agar-agar and apple juice in large saucepan. Bring to boil, reduce heat, and simmer for 10 minutes, stirring occasionally until agar-agar is dissolved.

Pour mixture into large bowl and chill for 1 hour or until firm. Purée chilled mixture in blender, gradually adding vanilla, lemon juice, almond butter, and soy milk. Blend until smooth.

Pour into 6 bowls or glasses and chill for 1 hour.

Mix blueberries with maple syrup, stirring and slightly crushing the berries. Remove mousse from refrigerator and top with blueberries and almonds.

6 servings

CAROB BROWNIES

4 ounces unsalted soy margarine

¼ cup honey

¼ cup maple syrup

1 teaspoon vanilla

⅓ cup carob powder

1 cup carob-flavored soy milk

2 cups whole wheat flour

1 cup rice flour

¼ teaspoon baking powder

¼ cup chopped nuts

¼ cup sweetened coconut, grated

Preheat oven to 350 degrees.

In a large saucepan, melt margarine at low heat and add the honey, syrup, vanilla, and carob powder. Stir until smooth. Remove from heat and stir in soy milk.

In a bowl, sift together flour and baking powder. Stir lightly into carob mixture, taking care not to overmix. Fold in the nuts and coconut. Pour into a lightly oiled and floured 8-inch square baking pan and bake for 35 minutes. Let cool before cutting.

Makes about 16 brownies

PINEAPPLE SHERBET

1 cup crushed pineapple

2 cups soy milk

2 teaspoons canola oil

⅛ cup raw sugar

¼ teaspoon natural vanilla

dash real salt

Combine pineapple with 1 cup of the soy milk and 1 teaspoon of the oil, plus all other ingredients, in a blender. Blend until smooth, then add remaining soy milk and oil. Blend again, chill, and serve.

4 servings

PUMPKIN PIE

2 cups pumpkin, cooked and mashed
(sweet potatoes or butternut squash may be substituted
for the pumpkin)

1 cup soy milk

¾ cup raw sugar

¼ cup cornstarch

3 tablespoons canola oil

1 tablespoon molasses

1 teaspoon cinnamon

½ teaspoon nutmeg

¼ teaspoon powdered cloves

1 unbaked pie shell

Preheat oven to 450 degrees.

Combine the pumpkin with soy milk and sugar; mix in oil and molasses.

In a separate bowl, mix together the cornstarch, oil, molasses, and spices, then combine with the wet ingredients.

Pour into unbaked pie shell and bake at 450 degrees for 10 minutes, then reduce heat to 350 degrees and bake another 50 minutes until filling is firm. Serve with tofu whipped topping (see recipe in this section).

8 servings

TOFU CHEESECAKE

3 cups soft tofu

¼ cup lemon juice

½ cup canola oil

1 cup raw sugar

1 teaspoon natural vanilla

dash real salt

1 prebaked pie crust

Blend all ingredients in blender until smooth. Pour into pie crust and chill. Serve with fresh berries or whipped tofu topping (see recipe in this section).

TOFU SHAKE

10 to 12 ounces soft tofu

raw sugar to taste

FOR FLAVORS, CHOOSE FROM:

1 cup frozen strawberries, thawed

1 ripe banana

1 cup canned crushed pineapple, with juice

1½ cups fresh-squeezed orange juice

Mix tofu and sugar in blender with flavor of choice and whip until smooth. Mix in some crushed ice or chill for a cool, refreshing, protein-packed drink.

1 serving

TOFU WHIPPED TOPPING

1 cup soft tofu

¼ cup canola oil

2 tablespoons raw sugar

1 tablespoon lemon juice

1 teaspoon natural vanilla

dash real salt

Blend all ingredients until smooth and creamy. Whip a little just before serving, and use as you would whipped cream.

VANILLA MILKSHAKE

4 cups soy milk

2 or 3 ice cubes

⅓ cup raw sugar

2 tablespoons canola oil

1½ teaspoons natural vanilla

dash real salt

Combine all ingredients in blender and blend well. Serve immediately.

2 servings

Index